CW00428307

One Foundation

**'Therefore, since we are receiving a kingdom
that cannot be shaken, let us be thankful ...'**
Hebrews 12:28

Selwyn Hughes
Revised and updated by Mick Brooks
FURTHER STUDY: IAN SEWTER

© CWR 2012. Dated text previously published as *Every Day with
Jesus: The Unshakeable Kingdom* (May/Jun 2002) by CWR.
This edition revised and updated for 2012 by Mick Brooks.

CWR, Waverley Abbey House, Waverley Lane, Farnham, Surrey GU9 8EP, UK
Tel: 01252 784700 Email: mail@cwr.org.uk
Registered Charity No. 294387. Registered Limited Company No. 1990308.

Unless otherwise stated all Scripture quotations are from the Holy Bible,
New International Version. © International Bible Society.

Cover image: Getty/Stone/John Humble
Quiet Time image: sxc.hu/John Nyberg
Printed in England by Linney Print

MIX
Paper from
responsible sources
FSC® C015900

ry Day with Jesus is available in **large print** from CWR. It is also available on **audio and DAISY**
he UK and Eire for the sole use of those with a visual impairment worse than N12, or who are
istered blind. For details please contact **Torch Trust for the Blind**, Tel: 01858 438260.
ch Trust for the Blind, Torch House, Torch Way, Northampton Road, Market Harborough, LE16 9HL.

A word of introduction ...

When Selwyn began to write this issue back in 2001, it was to focus on an entirely different topic. Then the world held its breath as the drama of the terrorist attacks of 9/11 took place. He immediately abandoned his original plans and turned his attention to the more relevant subject of the unshakeable kingdom of God. In his introductory letter to the issue, he wrote: 'I don't know how you felt at the time the tragedy took place but I would like to share with you briefly my own reactions. First, I felt shock and anger that something so terrible could be done by people in the name of religion. Second, a deep feeling of compassion for the victims and the loved ones they left behind. Third, a strong sense of joy and gladness that I belong to a kingdom that not even the most powerful bomb or missile can shake, let alone demolish.'

A decade on we are still living in a world of uncertainty and turmoil. Access to daily or even hourly news updates feeds the fear in our hearts. So it seems appropriate to re-release this particular *Every Day with Jesus*. Selwyn went on to say: 'Who knows what will happen in the years that lie ahead? ... My prayer is that you will find a new energy pouring into your soul as you consider again the fact that the kingdom into which we as God's people have been established is one that will never fall and one that will never end. It means everything to belong to such a kingdom.'

Sincerely yours, in His name

Mick

Mick Brooks
Consulting Editor

The one sure foundation

FOR READING & MEDITATION - HEBREWS 12:14-29

'Therefore, since we are receiving a kingdom that cannot be shaken, let us be thankful ...' (v.28)

'Life', said the writer Oswald Chambers, 'is more tragic than orderly.' How true those words seem when considered in relation to world events taking place in these times. And, in an age when the kingdoms of this world are being shaken, how thankful we can be that we belong to a kingdom whose foundations can never be moved. That is the unimpeachable promise presented in our text for today – a promise that is to be the theme of this issue.

The letter to the Hebrews was written to help Jewish (or Hebrew) Christians understand the superiority of Christ over every other person or order in the universe. It seems that some of these Christians had become a little alarmed when they discovered that a great deal of their ancient heritage was about to pass away. The writer to the Hebrews points out, however, that the shaking of the old is but the prelude to the new, the rule and reign of God, and he encourages them to establish their faith upon foundations that cannot be moved.

This verse, given to the Jewish Christians to steady them in a time of testing and confusion, is a verse that we ourselves must hold onto at this present time when all around us the kingdoms of this world and the godless civilisations they have built up are being shaken. By 'kingdom' I mean any society or culture not founded on values that are in harmony with the moral design of the universe. It may not be a kingdom in the strict sense of the word but if it does not stand for absolute truth and justice it will shake. Where now are the great empires of Assyria, Greece and Rome? Gone – for they were built on shakeable foundations. It means everything to know that there is one unshakeable kingdom.

FURTHER STUDY

Psa. 46:1-11;
Matt. 7:24-29

1. Why can we be free from fear?

2. What was the difference between the two houses?

Heavenly Father, amid earth's shakeable kingdoms I stand with my feet in the one unshakeable kingdom. Passing events cannot shake me, for in You I am unshakeable. I am so deeply thankful. Amen.

Dethroned powers still rule

FOR READING & MEDITATION – 1 CORINTHIANS 2:1-16

'We ... speak a message of wisdom ... but not the wisdom ...
of the rulers of this age, who are coming to nothing.' (v.6)

The truth that we belong to an unshakeable kingdom must surely be one of the most steadying thoughts we can cling to at this time. I do not consider myself to be a prophet but I predict that in the days ahead we are going to witness the disintegration of many societies where absolute truth and moral order are not priorities. It is inevitable, for any society not established on principles in harmony with the universe is bound to collapse.

Yesterday we mentioned that the great empires of the past, such as those of Assyria, Greece and Rome, were established on ideals that were meant to last for thousands of years. But now they have vanished, for they were built on shakeable foundations. And what about the lesser empires, both personal and collective, which men have created? They too have proved shakeable, and have been destroyed. In the Moffatt translation today's text reads as follows: 'We do discuss "wisdom" with those who are mature; only it is not the wisdom of this world or of the dethroned Powers who rule this world ...'

FURTHER STUDY

Dan. 4:1-37

1. Why did Nebuchadnezzar's kingdom fall?

2. When was it restored?

How can a power rule and yet be dethroned? The answer is that any power not based on truth, integrity and righteousness is destined to fall. The universe has passed judgment on all such powers. Though for the time being they still rule, they are under the law of decay.

Professor Henry Drummond once said: 'If you seek first the kingdom of God and His righteousness you will still have to face problems, but if you don't seek first the kingdom of God then you will have nothing but problems.' We who stand in God's kingdom may sometimes shake as we witness the events taking place in today's world, but be assured of this: the kingdom will never shake under us.

My Father and my God, I am so grateful that I am a subject of Your kingdom. Your kingdom is my homeland, therefore I am at home in all lands. Blessed be Your holy name for ever. Amen.

What is God's kingdom?

FOR READING & MEDITATION – MATTHEW 3:1-12

'In those days John the Baptist came ... saying, "Repent, for the kingdom of heaven is near."' (vv.1-2)

Before we go any further in our meditations we must pause to consider what is meant by the term 'the kingdom of God'. In both the Old Testament and the New there is just one meaning: God's kingdom is His rule. The kingdom is the *rule* of God – anywhere. The kingdom is often referred to in Matthew's Gospel as 'the kingdom of heaven', and is also called 'my Father's kingdom' (Matt. 26:29) and 'the kingdom of Christ and of God' (Eph. 5:5). Always, though, the thought is of sovereignty rather than of territory and of the activity of reigning.

As we see from today's reading, it was John the Baptist who first announced that the kingdom of heaven was at hand. Very soon Jesus took over the proclamation of this message, as Matthew 4:17 tells us: 'From that time on Jesus began to preach, "Repent, for the kingdom of heaven is near."' Our Lord's proclamation of the kingdom, although following John's word for word, differed in two respects from that of His forerunner. First, John's call was for repentance because of the judgment that was to come. Jesus' announcements included that message also, but He was able to emphasise that He had come not only to condemn sin but to save us from it.

FURTHER STUDY

Isa. 9:1-7;
Matt. 21:28-32

1. What was prophesied of Christ?

2. What and where is God's kingdom?

Second, Jesus proclaimed the kingdom as something that was now present, manifested through His own Person and ministry. For instance, in Matthew 12:28 He says: 'But if I drive out demons by the Spirit of God, then the kingdom of God has come upon you.' Jesus' authority over evil spirits was evidence that the kingdom had arrived. The kingdom came in Him and with Him. And to belong to Him is to belong to the kingdom.

Blessed Master, I am thankful that I belong to Your kingdom but even more thankful that I belong to You. This personal relationship means more to me than anything. I am deeply, deeply grateful. Amen.

When tragedy comes

FOR READING & MEDITATION - 2 THESSALONIANS 2:13-3:5

'But the Lord is faithful, and he will strengthen and protect you from the evil one.' (3:3)

Since we live in a world that is being shaken we must have a clear idea of how to think about matters when tragedy comes. We have touched on this but there is much more to be said. Not everything that happens is in accordance with God's wishes. After the terrorist attacks on the USA in 2001 in which thousands perished, one person wrote to me and said that the outrage was the will of God. No, it was not His will. God could not will it in the sense that He intended it to happen. The attacks were in part a consequence of God's great gift of freedom without which we would not be people, but puppets.

FURTHER STUDY

Gen. 4:1-8;
Acts 16:16-34

1. How did God intervene in Cain's evil plans?

2. How did God's power control the outcome and not actions in Acts?

When God made us as free people – people who could love – there was some risk, for with freedom comes the option of turning away from love and turning instead to hate. Free agents can not only help each other but hurt each other. And, of course, as we know from the story of Adam and Eve, human freedom has been radically affected by sin. But now let me ask you: Would you rather live in a world where no one could either love or hate? Do you wish God had made us so that we were *not* free, so that we could never influence each other, could never be friends, never guide, comfort or help each other? Never love?

With our freedom comes the possibility of thwarting the divine purpose for our lives. Yet for some reason we cannot quite understand with our frail human minds, God preferred to give us freedom rather than retaining control. To our minds, power and control are so similar that they tend to merge. With God they are separate. He will not use His power to control our sinful actions. He will, however, use His power to control the outcome of those actions.

O Father, we stand in awe at the fact that You made us not as puppets but as persons. We have the freedom to work with Your purposes or against them. Help us to use our freedom aright. In Jesus' name. Amen.

CWR Ministry Events

PLEASE PRAY FOR THE TEAM

TE	EVENT	PLACE	PRESENTER(S)
ay	Bible Discovery Evening Class – Exile and Coming Home	Waverley Abbey House	Philip Greenslade
ay	Christ Empowered Living	WAH	Mick & Lynette Brooks
May	Discovering More about God's Story [Title TBC]	WAH	Philip Greenslade
May	Insight Day - Helping Families Heal	WAH	Andre Radmall
May– ne	Introduction to Biblical Care and Counselling	WAH	Angie Coombes, Richard Laws & the CWR Counselling Team
une	The God of Love in a World of Suffering	WAH	Michael Baughen
une	Managing Your Time	WAH	Andy Peck
une	Preaching with Colour	WAH	Andy Peck
24 June	Bible Discovery Weekend – Nothing Can Stop the Gospel	WAH	Philip Greenslade
une	Caring God's Way	WAH	Mick Brooks & Lynn Penson
une	Education ... A Christian Undertaking?	WAH	Robert Jackson
une – y	Marriage on Track	WAH	Andrew & Lynn Penson
une	Insight Day - Eating Disorders	WAH	Helena Wilkinson

ase also pray for students and tutors on our ongoing **BA in Counselling** gramme at Waverley and our **Certificate and Diploma of Christian unselling** and **MA in Integrative Psychotherapy** held at London School Theology.

For further details and a full list of CWR's courses, phone +44 (0)1252 784719, or visit the CWR website at **www.cwr.org.uk**

Jesus has suffered too

FOR READING & MEDITATION - JOHN 20:24-31

'... see my hands. Reach out your hand and put it into my side.
Stop doubting and believe.' (v.27)

Following on from what we said yesterday, just suppose that Adam and Eve had never sinned and declared their independence from God – had never spoiled this beautiful earth. What if men and women had always done the will of God and responded at every stage to the leading of their loving heavenly Father? The world would have been a wonderful place where character would have grown without discipline, where love would never have been linked with pain, where there would never have been any need for sympathy. But that is not the world we know now. Our world is a world that has been affected by sin.

FURTHER STUDY

Heb. 2:14-18;
4:14-5:10

1. Why did Jesus share our humanity?

2. Why can Jesus help and comfort us so effectively?

In the midst of the chaos that sin produces, however, we find God at work turning things to good, and doing so with a graciousness that, when recognised, takes our breath away. Never has anyone who has walked the flinty way found Him not to be a source of comfort and consolation whenever they have sincerely called upon Him. And remember: Jesus has Himself suffered in this world of sin. Men pierced Him with nails and strung Him up on a cross to die.

Tragically, some who are on the flinty path do not know how to turn to Him. Perhaps rebellion and independence in their hearts prevents them. But all who turn to Him find Him ready to pour His grace into their wounded hearts and transform evil into good. A Christian woman who lost her husband in the World Trade Center tragedy said: 'When the news broke that my husband had been killed, a terrible darkness descended on me. But a hand reached out to me in the darkness. It was rough with work at a carpenter's bench and pierced with an ancient wound.' Beautiful.

Lord Jesus, forgive us that when we pour out our passionate protests to You and ask why You let bad things happen to us, we are forgetting that You have suffered too. May Your wounds heal our wounds. For Your own dear name's sake. Amen.

So-called rulers

FOR READING & MEDITATION – MARK 10:35-45

'... those who are regarded as rulers of the Gentiles lord it
over them ...' (v.42)

Four days ago we observed that Paul spoke of the rulers of this world as 'dethroned Powers'. The words of Jesus found in today's text convey a similar thought. The translator James Moffatt renders them in this way: 'You know that the so-called rulers of the Gentiles lord it over them ...' Fancy calling the leaders of the mighty Roman empire 'so-called rulers'. Well, the years and the centuries have spoken against the hours, and the so-called rulers and their empire have perished.

But notice that Jesus contrasted His small group of disciples with those 'so-called rulers': 'Not so with you,' He said (v.43). What He was saying was this: 'You are called to be rulers (or leaders) too, but unlike the so-called rulers of the Gentiles you are to be leaders who rule by love.' Those disciples, who imbibed the spirit of their Master, have passed on to us thoughts and principles and teachings that have moulded, and still mould, civilisation. And those who build on those principles and teachings are citizens of a kingdom that can never be shaken.

Listen to the words of an American commentator given in the aftermath of the terrorist attacks on the USA: 'Maybe now those who form our foreign policy will wake up to the reality of old-fashioned diplomacy, integrity, and fairness rather than putting their trust in big armies. In other words, when other things fail maybe we will come round to seeing and practising the principles given by a great leader many years ago – the principles delineated in the Sermon on the Mount.' This commentator saw in the midst of the shaking the need to turn to the principles which belong to an unshakeable kingdom.

FURTHER STUDY

Isa. 9:6-7;
Luke 22:24-30;
John 13:1-17

1. How long will Christ's kingdom last?

2. What is Christ's model of leadership?

O Father, the more I reflect on this the more grateful I am that I belong to an unshakeable kingdom. Things may shake around me but nothing shakes inside of me. You are mine and I am Yours. Thank You, dear Father. Amen.

The only hope

FOR READING & MEDITATION – MATTHEW 13:18-23

'When anyone hears the message about the kingdom and does not understand it, the evil one comes ...' (v.19)

Yesterday I made reference to a commentator who said: '... when other things fail maybe we will come round to seeing and practising the principles ... delineated in the Sermon on the Mount.' Jesus taught about the kingdom frequently and with clarity but, as our verse for today highlights, many fail to understand the teaching, and the devil uses this misunderstanding as an opportunity to draw people further away from God.

Every person longs to find meaning and purpose. Without this, the different parts of their lives feel like loose ends – compartmentalised. People want a goal, something to aim for, to aspire to, something on which to pin all their hopes, desires and dreams. Many corrupt political systems and ideologies have within them men and women who, in searching to find something on which to build their lives, have hit upon something which has no real foundations. They are searching for wholeness, but they find only more brokenness. They are searching for a just society but, in finding justice for some, others are disenfranchised. They trust their leaders, but find the leaders will use their followers' loyalty to serve their own ends. They are searching for the kingdom of God, but are not aware of it.

FURTHER STUDY

Dan. 7:15-28;
Acts 5:29-39

1. What characterises earthly kingdoms?

2. Why is the kingdom our only hope?

Doesn't this explain the driving force behind so many of the revolts and campaigns taking place in our world? People are searching for the kingdom of God without being aware that they are doing so. Dare we hope that in the shaking that takes place from generation to generation men and women will come to see that their only hope is to belong to a kingdom that is immovable – the unshakeable kingdom of God?

Loving heavenly Father, at this critical time in our world's history may Your Holy Spirit be at work showing men and women that their hearts will find rest only when they believe in Your unchanging Son and His unshakeable kingdom. Amen.

The Servant King

FOR READING & MEDITATION - 1 CORINTHIANS 15:20-28

'Then the end will come, when he hands over the kingdom to God
the Father after he has destroyed all dominion ...' (v.24)

The other day we noted that the thought expressed in the word 'kingdom' is the rule of God – anywhere. However, before the rule of God is finally re-established throughout the universe it will pass through various stages.

In the beginning, and before sin entered the universe by way of Satan's rebellion and Adam's transgression, God ruled over His universe with unhindered authority. The downfall of Satan, and Adam's failure in the Garden of Eden, however, brought about a cataclysmic tear in the universe which has affected every aspect of God's creation. Sin poured into the earth which has taken its toll on all forms of life, reaching deep into the animal, vegetable and mineral kingdoms. The truth is that although God originally set up the universe with Himself as its rightful King, the earth has, by reason of Adam's sin, become a revolted province. The dominion which God gave man in the beginning (Gen. 1:26) has now passed into the hands of Satan, and God's great design and desire is to once again bring the earth and its inhabitants into submission, peaceful and agreed co-operation with His rule and reign.

Despite the rebellion in His universe, God is pursuing an overarching purpose which involves the re-establishment of His kingdom throughout the whole earth by means of the personal intervention of His Son, the Lord Jesus Christ. In order to get a glimpse of God's plan we must span the ages from the beginning of time to its end, and see that the rule of God, broken in Adam, is to be re-established in Jesus Christ. And for that purpose the King of kings became the Servant King.

FURTHER STUDY

Isa. 14:12-15;
Ezek. 28:12-17;
Phil. 2:5-11

1. What was Satan's original position?

2. Contrast the attitudes of Satan and Jesus?

O God, how thankful I am that although the first Adam failed to do Your will, the last Adam - my Lord Jesus Christ - has succeeded. And in Him the future is for ever fixed. My gratitude is Yours for all eternity. Amen.

The truth kept alive

FOR READING & MEDITATION – ISAIAH 37:14-20

'O Lᴏʀᴅ Almighty ... you alone are God over all the kingdoms
of the earth.' (v.16)

We continue considering the various stages through which the kingdom of God has to pass, starting with sin entering the world and culminating with the day when God's rule will once again be universally re-established. In the beginning God's order was called into question by man's sin, and the result was chaos. God, however, instead of crushing this revolt by force, allowed it to pursue its course and consequences, but also put into operation a plan which would one day bring the universe back into harmony with Himself and, at the same time, demonstrate His own eternal love and true character.

FURTHER STUDY

Psa. 2:1-12;
1 Kings 10:4-29

1. What is God's response to human rebellion?

2. How is Solomon's reign a pattern of God's kingdom?

In the Old Testament we find a pattern for kingship, giving us an idea of what life can be like when a king and his subjects live together in harmony. Sadly, however, many of the kings of Israel and Judah were unrighteous and fell far short of God's ideal. So, through the prophets, God announced that one day the King of the universe Himself would come into the world to re-establish His kingdom in the hearts of His subjects.

All confusion about the kingdom disappears when we consider the orderly progression of teaching in the Old Testament which leads to the fact that the kingdoms of earth, though faint portrayals of heavenly things, were totally inadequate to produce universal peace and happiness. At each stage of history in the Old Testament we see events pointing like a signpost to the future, telling in types, pictures and illustrations that one day the King of heaven would appear and establish His rule in the hearts and minds of men. Now that day has come and the promised kingdom is ours. How wonderful! How truly wonderful.

O God, how unhurried You appear to be in Old Testament history. Yet I see that each period is a visual aid letting the world observe the unfolding of Your eternal purposes. How wise and wonderful are Your ways. Thank You, dear Father. Amen.

FOR READING & MEDITATION - HEBREWS 11:1-10; JOHN 14:2

'... he was looking forward to the city with foundations, whose architect and builder is God.' (11:10)

Ever since Adam forfeited his rights in the Garden of Eden, humankind has been afflicted with a sense of lostness. We stand as orphans in the midst of a bewildering universe, desperately trying to gain our equilibrium. In *The Message* version we find these words used of those who admit they are aliens and strangers on earth: 'they are looking for their true home' (Heb. 11:14). What a lovely description of the kingdom – *true home*. It conjures up a picture of safety and security, of belonging.

Philosophers down the ages have claimed that in order to understand the mysteries of life on this planet we must have a world-view of things, a universal framework which gives validity to all we think and do. The breakdown of this sense of world order is the cause of our inner lack of security, and is best defined by what someone has called 'the homesickness of the soul'. What we do seems to have little relation to the whole. This makes life empty and insecure. It is a fact that many of the young people in detention centres come from dysfunctional families. The framework in which they lived has broken down, and consequently they have become confused.

From the moment humankind was separated from its true home in the beginning we have needed a new home and a new universal framework which can give genuine understanding to all we think and do. In Jesus we not only have the promise of being reunited with the Father but we also have the guarantee of a new home which He Himself has gone to prepare for us. When we arrive in heaven I think the idea will grip us that here on earth we have never really been 'at home'.

FURTHER STUDY

Luke 15:11-24;
2 Pet. 3:9

1. Why do people reject their true home?

2. What is the Father's response to those who reject Him?

O God, how thrilling it is to realise that I am no longer an orphan but a child of God through faith in Jesus Christ. Thank You for restoring me to my Father and my true home. In Jesus' name. Amen.

The cosmic loom

FOR READING & MEDITATION - COLOSSIANS 1:15-23

'He is before all things, and in him all things hold together.' (v.17)

We are seeing that the human race, having been made for the kingdom of God, is homesick and ill at ease until it finds its way back into it. The poet Edna St Vincent expressed this thought in this way:

Upon this gifted age, in its dark hour,
Falls from the sky, a meteoric shower
Of facts … they lie unquestioned, uncombined.
Wisdom enough to leech us of our ill
Is daily spun; but there exists no loom
To weave it into fabric.

FURTHER STUDY

John 1:1-10;
1 Cor. 8:6

1. Why can a framework for life only be found in God?

2. Why may people lack a cosmic loom?

'There exists no loom to weave it into fabric.' Isn't this why life lacks meaning for so many? They have no cosmic loom on which the unrelated facts of life can be woven into the fabric of total meaning. Hence, unsurprisingly, they are uneasy. The men and women of this age purposefully spend their time, energy and efforts on finding something to which they can give themselves – fully. They want something they can totally believe, in the hope that this will bring them total meaning. What we are all searching for really is the kingdom of God – we are homesick for our native land.

In my teens I sought for one thing after another to help dispel the sense of 'homesickness' that was in my soul. Then I heard the message of the kingdom, and when I received it I said: 'This is it! My search is over.' The kingdom of God became the cosmic loom on which I have been able to weave all the facts of life from that day to this.

Gracious Father, I am grateful that in Your kingdom I have found the cosmic loom which enables me to weave all the facts of life into one harmonious whole. I am so blessed. Thank You, dear Father. Amen.

The broken nest

FOR READING & MEDITATION – ACTS 17:22-31

'For in him we live and move and have our being.' (v.28)

We spend another day thinking about what happens to us when we lose the big picture view of things. Yesterday we recognised that human beings, having been designed for the kingdom of God, are hopelessly confused when they live against the grain of the universe. God's design for the world is that His will should be done on earth as it is in heaven, and when it is not then life breaks apart. Is this not the root cause of meaninglessness and emptiness that lies deep down in every human heart?

The Chinese have a saying that goes like this: 'In a broken nest there are no whole eggs.' Because the 'nest' of life has been broken by Adam's sin, our centrality and unity is fractured. There is just no way that we can handle ourselves confidently with poise and power in this vast universe without a sense of being linked to the kingdom of God. As we also noted two days ago, many juveniles in detention centres come from dysfunctional families. The framework in which they lived has broken down, often leaving them inwardly confused and bewildered. Our true home is the kingdom of God, and until we find it we too will be bewildered and live like orphans in the world.

FURTHER STUDY

Prov. 27:8;
Jer. 2:5-19

1. What two sins did God's people commit?

2. What happens when we break our God-given nest?

Over one of the doors in a theological seminary I once visited in the United States the following words are inscribed for all to see: 'Harmony of sound is music; harmony of colour is art; harmony of life is the kingdom of God.' In all God's communication with the human race since the Fall the dominant theme is the need to again enter into correspondence with the environment for which it was made – the kingdom of God. Outside it we are like cut flowers – living, but without roots.

O Father, day by day the truth is dawning on my spirit that only as I live my life in accordance with the laws of Your kingdom can I find the harmony for which my whole being craves. I am so thankful I have found it. Amen.

WHO CAN HELP CHANGE THIS MAN ...

BUT THE MAN WHO JESUS CHANGED?

Many an imprisoned offender longs to change, yet fears he never can ... fears that his old life on the 'outside' will always send him back 'inside'. And the hope that prison chaplains speak of, he fears is not for him. Hope? They've not led the life he has ...

Yet ... introduce him to a man who's risked that leap of faith himself - a once-lost man, now found - a man brought out from darkness by this Jesus - that's a man he'd follow and listen to.

There is such a man: the Hell's Angel become God's messenger, the reformed hell-raiser Brian Greenaway. Greenaway knows all about the the poisonous anger seething inside - and he's written a book about it called *The Monster Within*.

This is a shocking record of Greenaway's early life of rejection, violence and imprisonment and then the joy of his redemption when he invited Jesus into his life. Never before had Brian encountered the pure love of God, and he writes in his book:

'Instantly I felt all the rottenness and poison inside me leave. All the frustrations and anger that had kept me locked away for the greater part of my life disappeared. At the same time it seemed a window opened in my head and the love of God streamed in.'

Brian's book is a road map for those who are lost as he once was – a road map leading them to the spiritual and emotional freedom Jesus brings.

Thanks to our links with the Prison Chaplaincy Service we plan to distribute 20,000 copies of *The Monster Within* to prisons and Young Offender establishments throughout the UK.

The chaplains – who have responded enthusiastically to our initiative and eagerly await delivery of their book consignments – are already identifying their most 'ready' recipients.

A gift of £24 from you today could fund the production and print of 40 books, £37 could pay the distribution costs for 150 copies. Any amount you can spare, however large or small, will help directly to free spiritually blocked lives.

Please use the GIFT TO CWR section on the order form at the back of this publication to send your donation today.

Christ's first message

FOR READING & MEDITATION – MATTHEW 4:17-25

'From that time on Jesus began to preach, "Repent, for the kingdom of heaven is near."' (v.17)

Over the past few days we have been attempting to discover what lies behind the term 'the kingdom of God', and we have seen that it means the rule of God – anywhere. We have seen also that because of humanity's failure to dwell contentedly in God's kingdom, He made clear the truth of His sovereignty through the events of Old Testament history. After close on 4,000 years of teaching and of preparation for the unveiling of His kingdom, the Servant King descends from His throne in the heavens and chooses to dwell on this rebellious earth.

FURTHER STUDY

Judg. 21:25;
Isa. 53:1-12

1. What happens when there is no true king?

2. What do each of us do?

Almost the very first announcement Jesus makes as He begins His ministry is this: 'Repent, for the kingdom of heaven is near.' Why does Jesus give such a clear message in His first approach to the human heart? The answer is that right away He comes to grips with the fact that the matter which called God's rule into question at the beginning was human insistence on the right to rule one's own affairs. So, if men and women are to be received once again into the kingdom of God then they must reverse this decision and admit to God's rule as being true.

The desire to resist God's rule and reign is deeply ingrained within each one of us, and it is this which makes us aliens to the kingdom of God. The heart is indeed a resistant rebel, and before we can discover what life is really like in God's kingdom we must repent of this innate desire to have our own way, agree with God and acknowledge His right to reign in our lives. We come into the kingdom not through evolution but by revolution; not through better birth but by the new birth.

Dear Father, help me to be free from this ingrained desire to have my own way, and show me even more clearly that it is only as I repent that I can be received into Your kingdom. In Christ's name. Amen.

Cultured or converted?

FOR READING & MEDITATION – MATTHEW 18:1-9

'... unless you change and become like little children, you will never enter the kingdom of heaven.' (v.3)

The thought with which we ended yesterday is that we come into the kingdom of God not through evolution but by revolution. There are some who feel that they can become part of the kingdom by exposing themselves week by week to the activities of the Christian Church and its teaching – salvation by osmosis. An Anglican friend of mine who was once a vicar in a very fashionable parish called such people 'cultured Christians'. They have all the appearance of being genuine children of God but they have never personally undergone the life-changing experience which the Bible calls conversion.

Why is it that so many struggle against Jesus' call to repentance as the prerequisite to entry into the kingdom of God? Is it not that the instinctive reaction of the human heart is to raise up barriers against an intruder? Jesus needs to be given back full access to our lives, and this, of course, runs diametrically opposite to the self-centred instinct which lies deep within us. We struggle to preserve our self-dependence, and avoid anything that challenges the pride principle that has entwined itself about our nature. We fear 'lest having Him we have naught else beside'.

Let there be no doubt about it: the only way into the kingdom of God is through repentance. When we repent of our sin, our independence, we allow God to bring us into His kingdom by the miracle of conversion. And what is conversion? Someone has defined it as 'the change, sudden or gradual, by which we pass from the kingdom of self into the kingdom of God'. We are not cultured into the kingdom; we are converted into it. We must be born again. Permit me as a friend to ask: has this happened to you?

FURTHER STUDY

John 1:12-13; 3:1-17; 1 Pet. 1:23

1. Why must we be born again?

2. How does it happen?

O God, help me to answer this question frankly and fearlessly. And help me know what it means to be a true Christian; not a cultured Christian, but a converted one. I surrender to You. In Jesus' name. Amen.

Receiving the kingdom

FOR READING & MEDITATION - HEBREWS 12:14-29

'... since we are receiving a kingdom that cannot be shaken,
let us be thankful, and so worship God acceptably ...' (v.28)

As I know that some of my readers are not yet Christians, I feel I must dwell on the issue I raised yesterday a little longer. Forgive me returning to Hebrews 12:28 for a second time – as I said earlier, it is one of the most steadying verses in the New Testament. And it answers so clearly the question: how do I join this community of the unshakeable kingdom of which the Scriptures speak?

Well, the wonder of it is that we don't have to strive to attain it – we simply receive it. 'Since we are receiving a kingdom … let us be thankful.' *Receiving* – notice that! We don't have to be deserving, worthy or even do anything. We simply have to *receive* the kingdom by surrendering our lives to the King. In other words, God is prepared to invite us and welcome us into the community of His kingdom providing we are willing to take down the barriers and allow His Son to enter into our lives. This is how we surrender; by taking down the central barrier of self-centredness and saying to Jesus Christ, God's Son: 'Come in and have Your way.' Then the kingdom possesses us.

FURTHER STUDY

Eph. 2:1-9;
Rom. 10:8-13

1. Why will 'works' not save us?

2. Outline the process of salvation.

When we receive the King then the laws of His kingdom begin to work in and through us. We become agents of forces not our own. And, lest anyone thinks that living in God's kingdom requires simply a slavish obedience to rules and regulations, let me make it clear that once we take down the central barrier of our unsurrendered selves then God's grace works in us enabling us to live according to His laws. We become transmitters of the grace of God in as much as we love with a love that is not our own, rejoice with a joy that is not our own, and are filled with a peace that is not our own.

O God, I see so clearly that to be invaded by You I need to take down the barrier of my unsurrendered self. I do so now - willingly and happily. Come and reign in every part of my being. In Jesus' name. Amen.

FOR READING & MEDITATION - COLOSSIANS 1:9-14

'For he has rescued us from the dominion of darkness and brought us into the kingdom of the Son he loves ...' (v.13)

At this point I feel I should move slowly and steadily as some of my readers may not yet have opened themselves to the love of God and entered into the kingdom of our Lord and Saviour Jesus Christ. We receive the kingdom by surrendering ourselves to the King of kings.

A missionary tells of holding a Christian meeting in Japan just after World War II. The Japanese empire had been shaken to the very dust, and many thronged into the large church which had been booked for the occasion to hear of a new and unshakeable kingdom. As the missionary approached the church he saw men standing in the dark at the various intersections holding lighted Japanese lanterns, with a cross on each one. These men were waving the lanterns to show people the way to the church, encouraging them by the lighted crosses to turn in and hear the Word of Life.

Right now we stand at one of the most critical intersections of human history. The age through which we are passing is one of the most complex periods of all time, and many are confused and perplexed. For many years now my main mission in life has been to lift up the cross of the Lord Jesus Christ and wave it, as did those Japanese with their lanterns, to help guide bewildered people towards the kingdom – the one unshakeable kingdom in a shaking world. The cross is the only way into that kingdom. When you kneel at the cross and surrender all that you have, then your feet will be firmly planted on the solid rock of the kingdom that will never be shaken.

FURTHER STUDY

Acts 2:36-41;
1 Cor. 1:18-25

1. Why is the crucifixion the key to our faith?

2. Why is it often misunderstood?

O God, I bow before Your cross in real repentance and deep surrender. As I receive You into my life come and establish Your unshakeable kingdom in my soul. Then I know I will be safe, secure and unshaken by passing events. In Jesus' name. Amen.

Naturally Christian

FOR READING & MEDITATION - LUKE 17:20-37

'... nor will people say, "Here it is," or "There it is,"
because the kingdom of God is within you.' (v.21)

We move on now to consider one of the most perplexing verses in the New Testament. What exactly did Jesus mean when He said to the critical and fault-finding Pharisees: 'the kingdom of God is within you'? If the kingdom of God is within us – in everybody, even the unchanged (these words were spoken to religious Pharisees who apparently had not experienced a change of heart) – then why the need for the new birth?

Most evangelical commentators say the thought that Jesus was intending to convey here was that the kingdom is spiritual and not visible. But is it possible that there is another interpretation? I wonder if the thought in Jesus' mind was this: God has written the laws of His kingdom not only in the outer framework of creation but in our inner constitution too. We are made to work in God's way for His laws are stamped within our being. If we rebel against these laws written deep within us then we have to suffer the consequences and to put up with whatever happens as we live against the great design.

FURTHER STUDY

Prov. 6:20-29;
1 Tim. 6:9-10

1. Why do adulterers sin against themselves?

2. How is greed a sin against ourselves?

In previous issues of *Every Day with Jesus* I have drawn your attention to this great statement made by Tertullian, one of the Early Church Fathers: *Anima Naturalis Christiana* – 'the soul is naturally Christian'. When we sin, we not only rebel against the laws of the kingdom which are summarised in the Ten Commandments but we also sin against the laws of the kingdom inscribed within us. Every one of us is sinful to the extent that not only do we sin against the God who made us but we sin against the laws of the kingdom written in the texture of our being – we sin against ourselves and then face the consequences.

Gracious Father, You have written Your laws so deeply within me that when I run from You I run against the very grain of the universe. Help me to run with You for then I shall be free for ever. In Christ's name. Amen.

The insanity of sin

FOR READING & MEDITATION – GENESIS 1:26-31

'God saw all that he had made, and it was very good.' (v.31)

Today we continue reflecting on the verse we looked at yesterday, a verse which has been the subject of much debate in the Church down the centuries: 'the kingdom of God is within you' (Luke 17:21). When Jesus uttered those words He voiced an important truth. This truth has seldom been emphasised by evangelicals for fear of giving the impression that salvation is already ours. Though I appreciate that concern I do not share it. And the reason I do not share it is that I believe, with Tertullian, that the soul is naturally Christian.

If Tertullian is right then our inner being has been designed to function in a Christian way. That being so, we can easily see that to sin is not only to resist the rule and reign of God but to rebel against ourselves also – to work against ourselves in futility and frustration. God's ways are not simply written in the texts of Scripture but in the texture of our spiritual and physical beings also. God's ways, inscribed on the texture of our constitution, are self-authenticating. One doesn't need to argue for them; when we live against them they argue for themselves.

Listen to what my spiritual mentor, Dr E. Stanley Jones, said about this: 'Sin is not the nature of our being; it is against nature – our nature – and against the God who made it.' How I wish the contemporary Christian community would reclaim this verse rather than avoid it. If the kingdom of God is within us, written into the constitution of our being – the way we were made to live – then when we sin we not only cut ourselves off from God but we cut ourselves off from our own potential. We disrupt ourselves, our future, our all.

FURTHER STUDY

1 Sam. 15:24-26; 18:5-9; 1 Kings 21:1-19

1. How did Saul's sins disrupt him and his future?

2. How did Ahab's covetousness disrupt him and his future?

Father, I see that though sin is rebellion against You, and that this is the worst aspect of it, it is rebellion against myself also. How clear it is to me now that sin is insanity. Deliver me from all sin, dear Father. Amen.

The laws of the kingdom

FOR READING & MEDITATION - MATTHEW 5:1-12

'Blessed are the poor in spirit, for theirs is the kingdom of heaven.' (v.3)

You may remember that earlier we quoted a commentator, speaking shortly after the terrorist attacks on America: 'Maybe now those who form our foreign policy will wake up to the reality of old-fashioned diplomacy, integrity and fairness ... In other words, when other things fail maybe we will come round to seeing and practising the principles given by a great leader many years ago – the principles delineated in the Sermon on the Mount.' This commentator saw in the midst of the shaking the need to practise principles which belong to an unshakeable kingdom. Basically there are eight of them, and it is to the first of those principles that we turn now.

FURTHER STUDY

Exod. 20:3;
Prov. 16:18;
Ezek. 31:1-14

1. How does the first commandment relate to the first beatitude?

2. How does pride arise and what is the result?

'You're blessed when you're at the end of your rope. With less of you there is more of God and his rule' (v.3, *The Message*). The principle of humility is presented first because unless we come to grips with this then the others are beyond our reach. When sin struck deep into the human spirit the first effect was to remove God from the centre of our beings, and when God is no longer the centre then we become the centre – we take God's place. Eugene Peterson paraphrases part of Deuteronomy 4:25 in this way: 'When the time comes that you ... start taking things for granted, if you then become corrupt and make any carved images ...' When we take God's presence for granted then we corrupt ourselves by making carved images – and that image is usually ourselves. When we lose God then we put ourselves in His place. Such is the nature of human pride that it struggles to maintain self at the centre, and this produces self-centredness – the opposite of humility. No humility, no progress. That is the first law of the kingdom.

O God, baptise me with the power of Your Holy Spirit so that my self-centredness shall be overcome and You will once again become the centre of my life. In Jesus' name. Amen.

The downward path

FOR READING & MEDITATION – MATTHEW 27:3-10

'So Judas threw the money into the temple and left. Then he went away and hanged himself.' (v.5)

Consider what happens when humility is absent and self-centredness rules. A brief look at the life of Judas will show us the consequences of allowing self-centredness to hold sway. As far as we can tell Judas began his career as a disciple with loyalty, fidelity and passion, but he took a step downwards when he thought that one could give too much to Jesus. He objected to the lavish gift of a woman who, to his way of thinking, appeared extravagant in her love (John 12:5). Another step downwards came when he asked: 'What are you willing to give me ...?' (Matt. 26:15). Note: 'give me'. Third, the Scriptures tell us that 'he sought opportunity to betray him' (Matt. 26:16, NKJV). Judas tried to arrange things so that they would harmonise with his own self-centred plan.

When Judas saw that his plan was about to fall to pieces he 'repented' (Matt. 27:3, AV), but his repentance was unproductive because he turned back to the high priest and the elders instead of to Jesus. His repentance was no more than remorse, for he lacked a true desire to move away from self-dependency back to dependency on Jesus. The difference between repentance and remorse is this: repentance is the yielding of the heart to Jesus to be made clean; remorse is an emotion of self-disgust. Remorse causes one to eat one's heart out whereas repentance involves seeking a new heart.

Judas then tried to steady his tottering world by restitution: he returned the money. But he retained himself. The self that was so demanding now became impossible to live with so he hanged himself. He went against the grain of the universe and against the way God designed him, and he faced the consequences.

FURTHER STUDY

2 Sam. 17:1-23;
2 Cor. 7:8-11

1. Why did Ahithophel hang himself?

2. What is the difference between godly and worldly sorrow?

O God, I see so clearly that this imperious demanding self will push me outside the circle of Your purposes for my life unless I give it to You for cleansing and adjustment. I do so now – willingly and freely. In Jesus' name. Amen.

Humility - some wrong ideas

FOR READING & MEDITATION - JOHN 13:1-17

'... he poured water into a basin and began to wash his disciples' feet, drying them with the towel ...' (v.5)

Many have a wrong idea of humility. Once, after I had given a talk on humility, a woman commented: 'I did so enjoy your talk on humility. You see, it's the quality I most admire in myself.' At that moment I didn't have the heart to confront her over the issue, but what that dear lady thought was humility was really pride. In reality the humble do not realise they are humble; their actions and attitudes are as natural as breathing.

Jesus, knowing 'that he had come from God and was returning to God' (v.3), was able to take a towel and wash the disciples' feet. Because He knew who He was, and that His security and dignity rested with His Father, He was free to turn His energies away from Himself and use them to serve others. You can be humble only when you are conscious of being secure. Real humility is not rooted in a sense of humiliation but in a sense of being inwardly secure – in Jesus. People who carry an air of superiority are often suffering from a sense of littleness because little people don't dare to be humble; it would give away their littleness. They have to act a part – the part of being great – to compensate for being small. However, people who understand who they are in Christ don't have to act a part. They are secure knowing that they are 'accepted in the Beloved' (Eph. 1:6, NKJV), so free to express humility.

When we know who we are and understand our position in Jesus then we experience a sense of self-assurance without self-centredness. This prevents us from acting in a superior manner and enables us to be genuinely humble. An old proverb says it well: 'The little man is afraid to bend lest he expose his littleness.'

FURTHER STUDY

Luke 18:9-14; Phil. 2:1-11

1. What is God's promise to the humble?

2. How is humility linked to obedience?

O God, renew the vision of who I am in You so that no longer will I have to use my energies in developing my own sense of importance. Then I will be free to turn from serving self to serving others. Amen.

FOR READING & MEDITATION - MATTHEW 5:1-12
'Blessed are those who mourn, for they will be comforted.' (v.4)

Now we come to the second of the kingdom principles: 'How happy are those who know what sorrow means, for they will be given courage and comfort!' (v.4, Phillips). One Welsh scholar worded it in this way: 'Blessed are those who have allowed God to break their hearts, for through it they will become more sensitive to the needs of others.'

Have you ever wondered why God allows you to go through distressing experiences? One answer is found in Paul's second letter to the Corinthians: 'He comes alongside us when we go through hard times, and before you know it, he brings us alongside someone else who is going through hard times so that we can be there for that person just as God was there for us' (2 Cor. 1:4, *The Message*). As a Christian counsellor I have talked with many people who have stumbled over the fact that God allows troubles and trials to invade our lives. However, once they have come to see that God permits pressure for a purpose, then they have experienced a sense of release. If we shrink from the difficulties and seek to be free of the irritations, we may deprive ourselves of the potential benefits, but if we respond with expectancy and an open heart and mind then we will allow God to achieve His highest purposes in us.

FURTHER STUDY

2 Cor. 1:3-11;
7:5-7;
Gal. 6:2

1. What good may come from pressure?

2. How can we bear others' burdens?

The Living Bible's paraphrase of some words from Paul's second letter for the Corinthians is beautiful and helpful: 'What a wonderful God we have – he is ... the source of every mercy, and the one who so wonderfully comforts and strengthens us in our hardships and trials. And why does he do this? So that when others are troubled, needing our sympathy and encouragement, we can pass on to them the same help and comfort God has given us' (2 Cor. 1:3-4).

Lord, I have had my life strategy all wrong and have become tangled up because of my resistance to Your pressures. From today I will receive everything You send, not with a grumble, but with gratitude. Amen.

Going for Gold

With the 2012 Olympic Games fast approaching, CWR introduces a summer programme of training to build your spiritual muscles, as well as two new publications to spur you on in the race of life!

KEEP UP THE TRAINING

CWR has recognised that of the many people visiting the UK for the Olympic Games, there will be some who would like to take the opportunity to visit our headquarters and training centre, Waverley Abbey House, only a one-hour train ride from London Waterloo. To enable you to make the most of a visit to us, we have arranged a full and varied programme ...

Woman to Woman
Mon–Fri 16–20 July
This unique course is designed for women of all ages who want to help and minister to other women, whether on a one-to-one basis, leading a small group or with responsibility for a church or area-wide group.

Refreshing your View of the Bible
Mon–Fri 23–27 July
This course will give you an understanding of the overall message of the Scriptures, how God has used the authors to communicate His truth and, crucially, what it says to us in the twenty-first century.

Introduction to Biblical Care and Counselling
Mon–Fri 13–17 August
If you have a heart to help others but are wondering how, then this five-day foundation course is ideal. You will be helped to reflect on your own life in the light of the biblical model presented, before using the principles to help others.

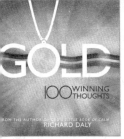

INSPIRING CHAMPIONS

The first of our new publications is a devotional book entitled *Gold*. Richard Daly has written 100 inspirational thoughts on taking part in the race, the journey, which is our Christian life.

Gold by Richard Daly
ISBN: 978-1-85345-665-7
£4.99

Next is *Professor Bumblebrain's Absolutely Bonkers Champions*! The star of our much loved *Professor Bumblebrain* series of children's books is back, this time with a full-colour comic on what it takes to become a true champion for God.

Professor Bumblebrain's
Absolutely Bonkers Champions
by Andy Robb
ISBN: 978-1-85345-656-5
£8.99 per pack of 10
Ideal for church and group resources

SHINING BRIGHT

We hope that something in this offering of publications and resources will appeal to you, as you consider your own Christian 'race' or how you can reach out to others with the good news of Jesus.

For full details of the courses opposite/to book,
visit www.cwr.org.uk or call +44 (0)1252 784719

The welcome mat

FOR READING & MEDITATION - JAMES 1:1-8

'Consider it pure joy, my brothers, whenever you face trials
of many kinds ...' (v.2)

The first time I read today's text in the Phillips translation I thought the translator had made a serious mistake, but when I checked it out with a friend who is a Greek scholar I discovered it to be absolutely correct. This is what it says: 'When all kinds of trials and temptations crowd into your lives, my brothers, don't resent them as intruders, but welcome them as friends!' In other words, when trials and trouble come your way, put out the welcome mat! And why should you do this? Because you 'Realise that they come to test your faith and to produce in you the quality of endurance' (v.3, Phillips).

FURTHER STUDY

Rom. 5:1-5;
Prov. 17:3;
1 Pet. 1:3-9;
4:12-19

1. What does suffering produce?

2. Why may we experience suffering?

Many Christians feel that they are entitled to some kind of protection from the adversities of life, but this is not so. Jesus said: 'In this world you will have trouble. But take heart! I have overcome the world' (John 16:33). We should never be surprised at the number of problems we face. Rather, we should remind ourselves of God's promise that He will never allow one single problem to come our way without making sure that we have the grace or strength to handle it. And because of this Christians are to welcome trials as they would welcome a long-lost friend.

Most Christians will admit that they fail in this regard, for instead of rejoicing when troubles come they rejoice when troubles go. When we meet our troubles head on and with thankful hearts then we immediately rob them of their power to harm us. One person has remarked: 'A Christian is like a tea-bag; he [or she] is not much good unless they have gone through hot water.' Hold on to this: the troubles you are going through are worth more than the cost.

Blessed Lord, help me to be willing to greet trials as friends. If I can adopt this attitude then I may be able to avoid despair. Burn it into every part of my spirit. In Jesus' name. Amen.

True survival value

FOR READING & MEDITATION - MATTHEW 5:1-13
'Blessed are the meek, for they will inherit the earth.' (v.5)

We look now at the third law of the kingdom: 'You are blessed when you're content with just who you are – no more, no less. That's the moment you find yourselves proud owners of everything that can't be bought' (v.5, *The Message*). The thought underlying these words is that of joyful submission to all God's demands, and an eager acceptance of His perfect will.

How we have shied away from the word 'meekness'. We have thought of meekness as weakness, and one writer claims that 'we have *purposely* misunderstood the word, for we have been afraid of what it would demand of the self, namely surrender'. For meekness is just that – surrender. When a scientist approaches the mysteries of the universe in a spirit of meekness he is able to harness the mighty forces that surround us to advantage. When a scholar approaches the world of thought and learning in this spirit he finds its richest secrets unveiling themselves to him. When we approach life in the same spirit of meekness and submission which Jesus exemplified in His own life then we discover the promise coming true that the meek will inherit the earth.

Those who are meek exhibit self-control (see Gal. 5:23). They are disciplined and bring themselves under the discipline of accepting the will of God in its entirety. The poet Robert Browning (1812–1889) said: 'Who keeps one end in view makes all things serve.' When that one end is the kingdom then all things serve those who serve the kingdom. Anger and impatience (the opposite of meekness), as Moses discovered, keep us out of the 'promised land'. Instead of settling down to all God has for us we wander in the wilderness of a self-imposed exile.

FURTHER STUDY

Num. 20:1-13;
Psa. 106:32-33;
2 Cor. 10:1

1. What rash words of Moses kept him out of the promised land?

2. How did Paul emulate Christ?

O God, help me to live by Your principles, and impress upon me the fact that anger and impatience are decaying forces. Only meekness survives. Amen.

The cause of anger

FOR READING & MEDITATION - COLOSSIANS 3:1-8
'But now you must rid yourselves of all such things as these:
anger, rage, malice ...' (v.8)

Yesterday we saw that when we submit ourselves to the rule and reign of the kingdom we discover that the truth works for us in powerful and positive ways. But what happens if we resist the truths of the kingdom? We then have to face the consequences, and those consequences can sometimes find expression in anger and impatience.

Have you ever considered what it is that drives Christians to be angry and impatient? These emotions arise whenever we lose sight of the fact that 'in all things God works for the good of those who love him, who have been called according to his purpose' (Rom. 8:28). Once we become aware of the fact that as heirs of God, and joint-heirs with Christ, we belong to God's own family, and that He will never allow anything to happen to us unless He can use it for good, then this conviction becomes the 'cosmic loom' on which all of life is woven. If we do not accept this fact then we will respond to life in negative ways, by becoming angry, frustrated and impatient.

In life we may encounter many situations which can produce anger, frustration and impatience. For example, when the job we have set our hearts on is given to another person. We may feel that we were the best qualified applicant, even that God has called us to the role. When we are not successful we can allow resentment and bitterness to build up, which has a negative effect on our wellbeing. When we respond to life with a simple trust that God will never allow anything to happen to us that will not work out for our good then anger and impatience will disappear from our hearts as surely as the morning mists are dissolved by the rays of the rising sun.

FURTHER STUDY

Eph. 4:25-32;
Heb. 12:14-15

1. How may the devil claim a foothold in our lives?

2. What may happen if we ignore God's grace?

Dear God, deepen the conviction in my heart that You will allow nothing in my life unless it can work for good. Flow into my heart with a special supply of Your Spirit this very day. In Jesus' name. Amen.

The effects of anger

FOR READING & MEDITATION - PROVERBS 16:19-33

'Better a patient man than a warrior, a man who controls his temper than one who takes a city.' (v.32)

At the moment we are considering the consequences of failing to live according to the laws of the kingdom, and we are seeing that anger and impatience are often the result of a failure to recognise that everything that happens to us can be used. There was a time not so many years ago when it was thought that to get angry and impatient was simply bad; it made people difficult to get along with, but that was all. But now, following research, the effects of this kind of lifestyle are being revealed. It takes its toll in all aspects of our lives.

The connection between one's stress level and one's health is undisputed. Blood pressure increases during a bout of stress or anger, and can still rise seven days later if the trigger point is remembered. Anger and elevated stress levels have been linked to a higher risk of heart disease and other health problems. Research suggests that hardening of the arteries seems to advance faster in people who score high in anger and hostility tests.

FURTHER STUDY

Psa. 37:1-11;
Eccl. 7:8-9

1. What will the meek enjoy?

2. Where does anger reside?

There are other physical symptoms which arise from anger and impatience, including: a tight throat, tension in the neck and back with the shoulders raised, shallow breathing, a rapid heart beat, cool but mildly perspiring hands and feet, tight leg muscles, clenched fists, a frowning face. If avoiding these symptoms is not incentive enough to live according to God's original design, I am not sure what else is! Medical research is making it quite clear that our bodies are made for good will, not bad will, and slowly but surely we are beginning to see that we are made in our constitutions to live by the laws of the kingdom, and that to live against them is both foolhardy and purposeless.

O God, now that I see the problems that anger and impatience bring, I am eager to turn from the problems to avail myself of Your power. I know that deliverance is at hand. Please help me to reach out and take it. Amen.

Do it anyway

FOR READING & MEDITATION - MATTHEW 5:1-13

'Blessed are those who hunger and thirst for righteousness,
for they will be filled.' (v.6)

We look now at the fourth law of the kingdom: 'You're blessed when you've worked up a good appetite for God. He's food and drink in the best meal you'll ever eat.' (v.6, *The Message*). The message here is that each one of us needs to have a healthy spiritual appetite for the things of God, which is developed through prayer, reading His Word and living by the principles of His kingdom.

One of the very first signs of spiritual ill health is avoidance of time spent before God and study of the Bible – things which are vital to our spiritual growth and development. When our relationship with God through prayer and the reading of His Word is intact then every other relationship is affected by it. I know of nothing that cultivates a spiritual appetite more than spending the first minutes of the day with God in prayer and in the study of the Scriptures. When I have what some call a Quiet Time then I experience a quiet heart, but when my Quiet Time goes then my quiet heart goes with it.

Some Christians struggle with this matter because although they know a daily Quiet Time is essential for their spiritual development, they lack the willpower to make time for it. It's rather like someone rapidly losing weight because of lack of appetite and being unable to remedy the situation because they just do not feel like eating. Doing what is necessary, even though you do not feel like it, is important not only to physical health but to our spiritual health also. Sometimes people say to me: 'But I don't feel like praying or reading my Bible every day.' My advice to such people is this: do it anyway. It may seem mechanical, but as you persist you will find it becoming medicinal.

FURTHER STUDY

Neh. 8:18;
Psa. 145:1-2;
1 Pet. 2:1-3

1. What were the practices of Ezra and the psalmist?

2. What should we crave?

Father, forgive me if I skimp on the time I need to spend alone with You. Help me be a more disciplined and dedicated person. In Jesus' name. Amen.

From creed to deed

FOR READING & MEDITATION - ACTS 17:10-15
'Now the Bereans ... examined the Scriptures every day ...' (v.11)

At present we are reflecting on the need to develop a healthy spiritual appetite through daily prayer and the reading of God's Word – the Bible. The question we are considering is this: do we wait until we feel like it to pray and read God's Word, or should we do so whether we feel like it or not? Our answer ought to be: we do so irrespective of our feelings. The Christian life involves more than a belief in certain doctrines; it requires a discipline which causes us to move beyond creeds – to deeds. The deed is really the creed – the thing we believe in enough to put into practice. What we do not believe in we do not practise. Those who go from week to week without establishing a daily discipline of prayer and Bible reading are severing themselves from the very life by which they grow.

'But how,' you ask, 'do we go about changing our feelings so that we want to pray and read the Bible?' First, review your life to see if there is anything that needs to be corrected. Is there some issue that needs to be put right? If there is, then attend to it at once. The old saying that 'sin will keep you from prayer, but prayer will keep you from sin' is right.

Second, recognise that there is nothing you can do to change your feelings. You cannot, for example, say to your heart 'feel happy', for the ability to change your feelings lies beyond your will. What you can do, however, is to exercise your will so that you keep your Quiet Time and, as you expose your thoughts to God in prayer and through the reading of His Word, your thoughts, opened up to God, will bring about a change in your feelings.

FURTHER STUDY

Dan. 6:1-16;
Mark 14:32-41

1. How is Daniel a role model for us?

2. Why did Peter disobey Jesus?

O God, help me to understand that I must not let my feelings control my will, but make my will control my feelings. In Jesus' name I ask this. Amen.

Turning the tables

FOR READING & MEDITATION - PSALM 149:1-9

'Let the saints rejoice in this honour and sing for joy
on their beds.' (v.5)

We must spend a little more time considering an important aspect of human behaviour, namely the way in which our feelings are influenced by our thoughts. We cannot by an action of our will command our feelings to change, but when we use the influence of our wills to marshal our thoughts towards prayer and the reading of the Scriptures we soon discover that thoughts exposed to God in this way begin to influence and change our feelings.

I stumbled upon this principle almost by accident many years ago. One evening I left my office feeling extremely tired, and because of this I was not looking forward to the drive home. Try as I would I could not bring about any change in my feelings. However, I began to meditate on the words of the psalm before us today, and as I did so I began to undergo a strange experience. After about 15 minutes of meditation I began to feel inwardly released and extremely happy. Soon my joy seemed to know no bounds and I began to laugh out loud. This proved to be rather embarrassing as each time I stopped at traffic lights I was conscious of people staring at me. Since no one else was with me in the car it must have looked as if I was temporarily insane.

FURTHER STUDY

Psa. 1:1-6;
Eph. 5:19-20

1. What are the benefits of meditating on God's Word?

2. What should we be doing always?

When I arrived home I pondered on what had been taking place and realised that as I had brought my thoughts in line with the Word of God through meditation, I had unknowingly tapped the very feelings which the psalmist experienced when he wrote that psalm. The Bible is inspired by God and is a powerful book. Indeed, we are told that 'the word of God is living and active' (Heb. 4:12). As we meditate God speaks to us and can completely transform our thoughts and our feelings.

O Father, yet again I pray that I might become a more disciplined person. Help me through meditation to tap into the power that is resident in Your Word. In Jesus' name. Amen.

'For His sake'

FOR READING & MEDITATION – MATTHEW 5:1-13
'Blessed are the merciful, for they will be shown mercy.' (v.7)

The fifth law of the kingdom is this: 'Happy are the merciful, for they will have mercy shown to them!' (v.7, Phillips). Life in the kingdom teaches that as we forgive all those who have hurt us so we carry no hurt, bitterness or resentment with us on the road to heaven.

After delivering a message on the subject of forgiveness in the city of Pusan, Korea, many years ago, my interpreter, a young Presbyterian pastor, said to me: 'Please help me to forgive the Japanese.' He then told me how, during World War II, some Japanese soldiers had raped and murdered his mother, and he frankly confessed that he still felt hatred and bitterness.

In response I told him of a story I had read concerning an Armenian girl who had been enabled to forgive a Turkish man. She and her brother had been attacked by some Turkish soldiers, and although she managed to escape over a wall, it was not before her brother had been brutally murdered before her eyes. She was a nurse, and some time later she realised that one of her patients was the very soldier who had murdered her brother. Her first feeling was one of revenge, but she quickly overcame this and nursed the man back to health. When he was well she told him who she was. In astonishment he asked: 'Why didn't you let me die?' 'I couldn't,' she said, 'for I am a Christian. My own Master forgave His enemies who crucified Him. And I do the same – for His sake.' 'Well,' said the hardened soldier, 'if that is what it means to be a Christian I want to be one.' The Korean pastor then found it possible to forgive. And so can you. It isn't easy, but it can be done – with Christ's help.

FURTHER STUDY

1 Sam. 24:1-22;
Matt. 5:38-48

1. How did David refuse vengeance and what was the effect on Saul?

2. How should we treat our enemies?

Heavenly Father, I surrender all hurt, all resentment, all desire for retaliation. From henceforth I will be free – free from corroding hate and cancerous resentment. Enable me, by Your grace, to do this. In Jesus' name. Amen.

For more on this issue of forgiveness, we would recommend *Insight into Forgiveness* by Ron Kallmier and Sheila Jacobs. See page opposite tomorrow's notes for further details.

Giving up resentment

FOR READING & MEDITATION - MATTHEW 6:9-15

'For if you forgive men when they sin against you,
your heavenly Father will also forgive you.' (v.14)

So vital is this matter of forgiving others that we must give it some further thought. You cannot live happily in the kingdom with resentment in your heart. Those who have been forgiven by God must learn to forgive others. And when they have done so they will find that they are no longer harbouring feelings of bitterness.

Some, however, rather than forgiving those who have hurt them, still hold on to resentment and bitterness even though they themselves have been forgiven. Why do they do this? The answer is, in part, because of a touchy 'unsurrendered' self. When we hold on to resentment it shows that we have a self that is oversensitive because it is unsurrendered to the will of God. It is important to understand this because it may help you to deal more effectively with the problem. So do not concentrate on the symptom – resentment – but go straight to the root cause: the unsurrendered self.

FURTHER STUDY

2 Kings 6:8-23;
Matt. 18:21-35

1. Contrast Elisha and the King of Israel.

2. What happens if we do not forgive?

Consider also whether or not your resentment or unwillingness to forgive is rooted in an imaginary slight or insult. For instance, when oversensitive people see two or three people they know locked in a private conversation it is easy for them to imagine they are talking about them, and so they read into a situation something that is quite false. Check your attitudes honestly and ask God to help you deal with this problem once and for all. Pray for those who have hurt you. Make it a rule that every time you think of someone who has injured you, you will turn your thoughts to prayer for them. Establish it as a habit and then forgiveness will become habitual. Once you practise forgiveness then you will have no more enemies for you will have no more enmity.

O God, I know that my attitude of resentment eats like acid into my soul. I ask You now to deliver me completely from every trace of resentment. In Jesus' name. Amen.

Insight into Life's Big Issues

Some of the subjects Selwyn touches on in this *Every Day with Jesus*, such as forgiveness, are explored in greater depth in our *Waverley Abbey Insight Series*. Throughout the year at Waverley Abbey House, 'Insight Days' are taught by experienced tutors on key current issues faced by individuals and families. Aimed at informing both sufferers and those seeking to care for or help others, topics include: addiction; anger; bereavement; dementia; depression; eating disorders; self-esteem; and stress, amongst others.

For full details visit www.cwr.org.uk/training or call +44 (0)1252 784719

An accompanying series of books are available, and the following three books relate especially to topics covered in this issue:

Insight into Forgiveness
Ron Kallmier and Shelia Jacobs
Discover through real-life case studies, biblical examples and personal insights how to live in freedom from the past.
ISBN: 978-1-85345-491-2 **£8.99**

Insight into Anger
Wendy Bray and Chris Ledger
Deal effectively with the potentially life-wrecking state of excessive anger with this highly practical approach.
ISBN: 978-1-85345-437-0 **£8.99**

Insight into Anxiety
Clare Blake and Chris Ledger
Understand the various forms of anxiety and gain skills and strategies to deal with them.
ISBN: 978-1-85345-436-3 **£7.99** (softback)

All prices exclude postage and packing and are correct at time of printing. These books are available from CWR online at **www.cwr.org.uk/store**, by phoning **+44 (0)1252 784710** or from Christian bookshops. (For international readers, please contact your local national distributor **www.cwr.org.uk/distributors**)

We *must* forgive

FOR READING & MEDITATION - LUKE 23:32-38

'Jesus said, "Father, forgive them, for they do not know
what they are doing."' (v.34)

Dr. W.E. Sangster says of our Lord's cry from the cross, recorded in today's text: 'To concentrate on this single gospel incident alone will teach us more of how to deal with resentment in our own minds than reading many volumes.' The 'first word from the cross' is one of the most moving ever spoken by Jesus. According to tradition this prayer leapt from the heart of Jesus as He was actually being nailed to the cross. It is probable that while the beams were still flat on the ground He was laid prostrate on the wood, and the nails hammered into His hands and feet, and that as the blood spilled from the open wounds His plea rose to the highest heavens: 'Father, forgive them, for they do not know what they are doing.'

FURTHER STUDY

Acts 7:54-60;
Eph. 4:32;
Col. 3:12-14

1. How did Stephen follow Jesus?

2. Why must we forgive?

But might you say: 'I cannot forgive like that! It is beyond my ability to respond in this way to those who have hurt me.' Well, you do not have to do so alone. He who lives in you will also love in you, and as you surrender your problem into His hands He will enable you to forgive the deepest hurt.

A missionary lady walking along the street close to the kerb in a city in Japan was seriously injured when her coat caught in the handle of a passing taxi and she was dragged for several yards along the street. In the hospital she begged the authorities not to prosecute the driver of the taxi, and asked specifically that his insurance cover should not be taken away. The taxi driver was so moved by her attitude that following her death he attended her funeral and became a Christian. This is how all the followers of Jesus are encouraged to deal with bitterness and hatred. There is no other way. We must forgive.

O God my Father, nothing that anyone can do to me compares with what men did to You. Yet You forgave them! As Your disciple I too must forgive. So I forgive every offence ever committed against me - in Jesus' name. Amen.

Inner harmony

FOR READING & MEDITATION - MATTHEW 5:1-13
'Blessed are the pure in heart, for they will see God.' (v.8)

Now we come to the next law of the kingdom: 'Happy are the utterly sincere, for they will see God!' (v.8, Phillips). The thought here is of the need to submit our motives and inner thoughts to God and to the Lord Jesus Christ.

It is in this area that many Christians come up against difficulty. Over and over again I have been asked to counsel Christians struggling with impure thoughts and immoral desires. This conflict in our thoughts and desires is one thing that often pushes us towards the darkness of depression, and is responsible for a great deal of mental and spiritual ill-health. When our motives and desires are not guided by the fruit of the Spirit, but run unchecked and free to focus on whatever they wish, it will not be long before our conscience begins to tell on us and cause us to be burdened by a sense of guilt. Those who have had wide experience in Christian counselling agree that moral impurity is a cause of spiritual conflict in the soul. I have found there are three main root problems that produce spiritual conflict: moral impurity; bitterness and resentment; and lack of clear life-goals.

FURTHER STUDY

2 Cor. 6:16-7:1;
Heb. 12:14;
James 4:8

1. Why should we seek to be pure?

2. How can we resist impure thoughts?

Is it possible to keep our thoughts and desires pure, to follow God's original design for our lives and be free from the guilt which going against Him brings? It is! Inner harmony is gained when we give our whole beings to the power of the Holy Spirit and the complete lordship of Christ. It is no use trying to fight impure thoughts and desires, because the energy you use to fight them will eventually exhaust you. Draw near to God and surrender them to Him. The act of surrender passes them from your hands into His. And He is much more able to deal with them than you.

Gracious Father, I am beginning to see that if I am to know spiritual freedom then the springs of my thought life must be controlled by You. Cleanse those springs by the power of Your Holy Spirit - this day and every day. In Jesus' name. Amen.

Dealing with guilt

FOR READING & MEDITATION - 2 CORINTHIANS 10:1-6

'... we take captive every thought to make it obedient to Christ.' (v.5)

There can be no doubt that if we allow our thoughts and desires to focus on impurity, before long a cloud of guilt will descend upon our spirits. This guilt is responsible for a great deal of spiritual dis-ease and, if unresolved, can bring about serious damage to our personalities. Some forms of psychiatry approach this problem by trying to persuade the person experiencing a sense of guilt that he is more a victim than a violator of his conscience, and that he needs to re-educate himself so that he can accept a lower value system. But the problem is not that God's standards are too high; rather, that our performance is too low. When we go against God's original design for us, or transgress God's laws in any way, then it is God's intention that we should feel guilt. 'Guilt', someone has said, 'is God's way of drawing our attention to the fact that we have broken one of His principles.' To paraphrase C.S. Lewis – it is God's megaphone to arouse us in our deafness. This guilt is not intended to drive us to despair but to draw us to Him for deliverance. Only God has the answer to guilt. (Please note that the type of guilt I am talking about here is not false guilt but real guilt – the guilt that arises from a refusal of and resistance to God's kingdom.)

FURTHER STUDY

Psa. 32:1-5;
51:1-19;
1 John 1:8-10

1. How did David deal with guilt?

2. How should we deal with guilt?

There are a number of different things we can do when we experience a sense of guilt. We can repress the guilt by attempting to persuade ourselves it is not there. We can suppress it and try to keep it under control. Or we can confess it to God, ask for His cleansing and forgiveness, and seek to live by His power in the future so that we are free from its control.

O God, alone I am no match for the power of evil that bubbles upwards in my thought life. Yet with Your help my thoughts can be tamed, and brought under Your control. Cleanse me and help me to live as You intend. In Jesus' name. Amen.

Controlled by passion?

FOR READING & MEDITATION - MARK 7:14-23

'For from within, out of men's hearts, come evil thoughts, sexual immorality, theft, murder, adultery ...' (v.21)

The matter we are considering together is how to gain control over immoral and unhelpful thoughts and desires. Many Christians find they have, at times, to wrestle with strong sexual thoughts and longings. Life seems very heavily loaded on the side of sex. Everywhere we look we are faced with sexual images. Such images are used widely in advertising to promote the sale of everything from holidays to bathroom fittings. Can we not make decisions regarding our purchases without sex being used to entice us?

Sexual desire is not wrong and, providing it is understood properly, it can be used to work for us rather than against us. Human sexuality is often equated with creativity, and it can be used for more than physical creation; it can be elevated to express its creative power in other areas too. The truth is that the sex drive can be sublimated – both within the marriage relationship and outside of it. The consequence of this is that there is still an opportunity for those who are denied the ordinary means of sexual expression. Some of the greatest work in the Church of Jesus Christ has been accomplished by those who, by choice or otherwise, have been denied the normal outlets for sex, and have directed this power into other forms of creative activity. This means that an individual's sexuality is not suppressed, but expressed – through a different channel.

Be cautious of doctors, psychologists or psychiatrists who advise promiscuity or self-abuse as a way of release from passions. Such advice is completely contrary to the teaching of the Bible and creates more problems than it solves.

FURTHER STUDY

Matt. 19:11-12;
1 Cor. 7:8-9,
32-38;
James 1:12-15

1. What is an advantage of singleness?

2. How may we harness our passions?

Lord Jesus, help me to understand all my desires and to drive them in the direction of Your purposes lest instead they drive me. I become either a servant or a master. Let nothing master me but You. Amen.

Burying our criticisms

FOR READING & MEDITATION – MATTHEW 5:1-13

'Blessed are the peacemakers, for they will be called sons of God.'
(v.9)

We come to the seventh law of the kingdom: 'You're blessed when you can show people how to cooperate instead of compete or fight. That's when you discover who you really are, and your place in God's family' (v.9, *The Message*). This word of Jesus deals with our relationships, and is a strong word to have done with all forms of criticism, condemnation and judgment of others. A critical attitude can often stem from jealousy, a sense of inferiority, or egocentricity. Sometimes criticism is given under the guise of helpfulness, with the comment: 'I am saying this in love.' Yet you feel the motive is not love, but anger. We often find fault with other people in order to cover up the faults we are conscious of within our own selves. If out of love for someone you are led to draw attention to an issue in their life then let love show through in your attitude to them.

FURTHER STUDY

Rom. 12:14-16;
Eph. 4:7-16,29;
Heb. 12:14

1. How can we live in peace and harmony?

2. Exactly how do we speak the truth in love?

As a result of my experience in Christian counselling I have discovered that you can tell people anything you like – providing you do so in love. When love is high then criticism is low, but when criticism is high then love is low. As God's children we must work at building up good relationships between ourselves and others, and learn to bury our criticism of others. In the nineteenth century a disgruntled preacher who did not like the attention being given to D.L. Moody asked during a committee meeting called to organise a crusade for the American evangelist: 'Has D.L. Moody a monopoly on the Holy Spirit?' Someone quietly replied: 'No, but the Holy Spirit does seem to have a monopoly on D.L. Moody.' Does the Holy Spirit have a monopoly on you? If He does then all traces of carping criticism should have died within you.

O God, You are boring deeper and deeper into me each day. Help me not to resist, for I want You to go right through me until the clear waters of the Spirit burst upwards in my being. In Jesus' name. Amen.

We are not judges!

FOR READING & MEDITATION – MATTHEW 7:1-5

'Do not judge, or you too will be judged.' (v.1)

We are considering the importance of building good relationships in the kingdom of God and are seeing that in order to do this we must learn to deal with our criticism and condemnation of others. One preacher said: 'When we are in the prosecutor's stand we cannot be in the witness box. If we are denouncing others then we are not announcing Jesus.'

During the many years I have been a minister and a counsellor I have dealt with hundreds of problems created by rifts between individuals, and I have discovered that one reason why people harbour grudges is because they are aware of some, and not all, of the facts relating to a problem. When all the details have been disclosed then this makes a tremendous difference to their understanding and, in consequence, to their willingness to forgive. Often to know all is to forgive all.

Long ago I decided that only God is big enough, good enough and wise enough to decide other people's destinies, and when I gave up attempting to be the judge of the world I found a release in my spirit which has stayed with me to this very day. At one time I used to go about judging others and trying to run God's universe for Him, but I broke down physically as a result. A wise friend advised me: 'Selwyn, stop trying to run the world and act the part of God.' I did – and I have never done so again. We have such limited knowledge of people and their motives that we are in no position to judge them. So stop playing the judge. It is not your role to play. Only God knows the motives which prompt people to act the way they do. Our task is to love everybody – and leave the judgment to God.

FURTHER STUDY

Rom. 2:1-5;
14:3-4;
James 4:1-12

1. Why should we not judge others?

2. What may a judgmental attitude indicate?

O Father, save me from the evil of criticism and condemnation, and pour into my heart the power of Your love, which sees all and understands all. In Jesus' name. Amen.

Is Christ divided?

FOR READING & MEDITATION – 1 CORINTHIANS 1:10-17

'Is Christ divided? Was Paul crucified for you?
Were you baptised into the name of Paul?' (v.13)

The matter of how we can overcome our criticism and follow Jesus' command to be peacemakers is such an important one that we must spend one more day considering it. In the church at Corinth certain groups had begun to emerge – one around Paul, one around Peter, one around Apollos, and another around Christ. Many of them had moved away from the centre – Christ – and begun to be centred in men. And this is always divisive.

Sadly, this spirit lingers in the Christian community right up to this present day. One person made the following comment: 'God has let down a rope from heaven for us to take hold of – that rope is Christ. But we have taken the end of that rope and unravelled it into strands. One group takes hold of a strand and builds a whole denomination around it. Each thinks he has the truth when all he may have is truths about the Truth – the truth in the rope, not the strand. And we will be surprised that when God pulls up the rope a lot of other people holding to their strands will come up too.' The fragmentation of the Church, which has been split into so many factions, denominations and streams, undermines our witness to the world we are trying to win. We must pray, work and do all that we can in a practical way to heal these divisions in the Body of Christ.

FURTHER STUDY

Judg. 20:11;
Ezek. 47:13-14;
Eph. 4:1-6

1. How is the Church like the tribes of Israel?

2. What is the basis of Christian unity?

An apocryphal story I once heard tells how a member of a group known as the United Brethren said smilingly to a gathering of Christians from different denominations: 'In heaven we are all going to be United Brethren.' In response a Quaker belonging to the Society of Friends said quietly: 'Well, if in the hereafter we are all going to be United Brethren, why not be "Friends" right now?'

O God, despite the divisions that still exist in Your Body, the Church, I dare to believe that You are healing the wounds and bringing cosmos out of chaos. Help me to work for unity everywhere I go. In Jesus' name. Amen.

Overcoming fear

FOR READING & MEDITATION - MATTHEW 5:1-13

'Blessed are those who are persecuted because of righteousness,
for theirs is the kingdom of heaven.' (v.10)

We come now to the eighth and last of the laws of the kingdom, which Peterson paraphrases in this way: 'You're blessed when your commitment to God provokes persecution. The persecution drives you even deeper into God's kingdom' (v.10, *The Message*).

A large number of Christians find great difficulty in accepting the inevitability of persecution, and because they have never accepted the fact that those who resist, ridicule and even reject Jesus and His principles will also reject them, they eventually become fearful and make compromises in their spiritual life. If you have never done so before, face the fact right now that if you identify yourself closely with Jesus Christ then the world will persecute you. It may be a little, or it may be a lot, but a close relationship with Christ will prompt non-Christians to treat you with a degree of hostility, rejection and persecution. Once you acknowledge this fact you are nine-tenths of the way towards overcoming the fear of witnessing and the compromise of your Christian standards.

FURTHER STUDY

Matt. 10:16-31;
John 15:18-16:4

1. Why did people persecute Christ?

2. Why will they persecute us?

Many followers of Jesus are not always strong witnesses because they tone down their Christian testimony so as to avoid hostility or persecution, and they end up achieving little. So fix this fact firmly in your mind: those who resist, ridicule and reject Christ and His principles will also resist, ridicule and reject you. Once you understand this then you are free to throw your whole weight on Christ and become so fully identified with Him that your Christian witness will take on a sharpness which will astonish you. When you lose your own identity and gain Christ's identity then you will start to make great progress spiritually.

Gracious heavenly Father, please don't let me miss the truth underlying this last law of the kingdom, for when I fully understand it my witness as a Christian will become more effective. In Christ's name I ask this. Amen.

Identifying with Christ

FOR READING & MEDITATION - GALATIANS 2:11-21

'I have been crucified with Christ and I no longer live, but Christ lives in me.' (v.20)

We ended yesterday by saying that when we surrender ourselves to God's great Word and begin to take on Jesus' character and values we will start to make great progress spiritually. This is what the apostle Paul did, as we see from our text for today. Some believers falter in their witness and compromise their Christian standards simply because they are trying to maintain acceptance from others and, at the same time, give some kind of testimony to the work of Jesus Christ in their lives. It just cannot be done.

When we are resisting rejection then our basic self-centredness comes to the aid of our fragile human ego and persuades us to hold back on certain actions, or sugar-coat the truth so that it is more attractive to those with whom we come in contact. But this is counter-productive. The strength of our Christian witness to the world comes from the fact that we closely identify ourselves with Christ in every attitude, action and thing we do – trusting God with the outcome. Like Paul we should be able to say: 'I am not ashamed of the gospel' (Rom. 1:16).

FURTHER STUDY

Rom. 6:1-11;
7:1-6;
Gal. 6:14

1. Did the cross slay us or save us?

2. How does dying with Christ release us from sin and compromise?

One Christian leader I heard shared with a large group of people something which he claimed had revolutionised his witness to the world. He said that whenever he was called upon to do or say something he knew was against his Christian faith he would respond with these words: 'I have committed my life to Jesus Christ and I am not able to do that.' That one statement, he claimed, had brought about major changes in his life and experience. Dwell upon it. It may be just what you need to begin a new approach in your attitude to what is at times a hostile, Christ-rejecting world.

O God, give me clear insight so that this truth I am meditating upon may become a new force in my life and experience. This I ask in Jesus' name. Amen.

FOR READING & MEDITATION - 2 TIMOTHY 3:10-17

'In fact, everyone who wants to live a godly life in Christ Jesus will be persecuted ...' (v.12)

For one last day we focus on the laws of the kingdom. We have been saying concerning the final one that those who are closely identified with Christ mirror Him to others; their lives are so filled with His beautiful attitudes that they silently judge the lives of those who are not His, and as men don't like to be judged they kick back in persecution. 'Society,' said one person, 'demands conformity. If you fall beneath its standard it will punish you. If you rise above its standard it will persecute you. It demands an average, grey conformity.'

The Christian is, of course, different. His whole life is tilted upwards so that his progress is towards heaven. But then, when he rises too far above the multitude, he becomes a target and tends to get hit. Dare we suggest that if we don't get hit perhaps it is because we are not high enough above the multitude? 'Woe to you,' said Jesus, 'when all men speak well of you' (Luke 6:26). If they do, possibly it is because we are too much like them!

But we must now ask ourselves: What is the outcome of being closely identified with Jesus Christ? Here is the answer: 'for theirs is the kingdom of heaven' (Matt. 5:10). Not only do we belong to the kingdom of God; the kingdom of God belongs to us. All the forces that hold together this mighty universe are at our disposal when we live according to the laws of the kingdom. When we throw ourselves at the feet of Jesus and become His willing followers then the wheel turns a full circle and we end up by participating in His reign on the throne. We give ourselves to Him and the result is that He gives back to us the right to rule over all the forces that are against us – in His name.

FURTHER STUDY

Luke 21:12-19;
Rev. 2:8-11

1. How should we respond to persecution?

2. What is promised to the persecuted?

Father, as I have surveyed these 'beautiful attitudes' of the kingdom I have longed to see each one worked out fully in my life. Make it possible, I pray. In Jesus' name. Amen.

'I love you big – this much'

FOR READING & MEDITATION – ROMANS 5:6-11

'But God demonstrates his own love for us ...' (v.8)

Having considered the laws of the kingdom we move on to think about the crucifixion and resurrection and their relationship to the kingdom. There is no room for sin in God's kingdom, and the death of Jesus is the price that had to be paid in order to separate people from their sins. Wherever pure love meets sin a cross of pain is set up. Love, by reason of its own nature, gathers to itself the sins and sorrows of the offender, and makes them its own. In a world where sin has caused so much chaos love is bound to bleed, for when God's love comes in contact with sin in the hearts and lives of those He loves then a cross of pain is the inevitable result.

FURTHER STUDY

John 3:14-17;
1 John 4:7-21

1. How has God proved His love for us?

2. How should we respond?

We ought never to forget that the cross was a part of God's plan long before it was lifted up in history, for Christ was 'the Lamb that was slain from the creation of the world' (Rev. 13:8). How do we know that there is an unseen cross in the heart of God? We look to Calvary and through the visible cross on that 'green hill far away, outside a city wall' we see the hidden cross lying deep within the heart of God – the God who allowed His Son to bear our sins (see 1 Pet. 2:24). The outstretched arms of the cross are the arms of God stretched out to gather us to His heart.

A prisoner converted to Christ wrote this just two days after his conversion:

'I love you big – this much,' a child will say,
And thrust his arms out wide;
So baby Christ grew up to love that way,
With outstretched arms He died –
'I love you big – this much.'

O God, as I look through the cross lifted up on Calvary I see another cross engraved upon Your heart. I am so grateful that You carried that cross on Your heart in eternity before Your Son carried it up the hill of Calvary. And it was all for me. Amen.

FOR READING & MEDITATION - JOHN 12:20-36

'But I, when I am lifted up from the earth, will draw all men to myself.' (v.32)

Today we reflect further on the impact of the crucifixion and its importance in re-establishing God's rule in the universe. Yesterday we saw that the cross was God's answer to the problem of human sin in that Jesus carried our sins in His own body on that tree (1 Pet. 2:24). The manner in which God opened the doors of His kingdom to us is utterly amazing. He could have overpowered our stubborn resistance to His will by brute force, and could have crushed our rebellion and resistance more easily than a bulldozer demolishes an anthill. Yet instead He chose to win us by His love.

As He hung there on Calvary's tree the Son of God demonstrated the depth of His love, and showed us that there was no length to which He would not go to draw us back into His glorious kingdom. The way He chose was costly. The opening of the gates of the kingdom was no easy achievement. Arnold Lunn satirises the liberal view of the gospel in these words: 'God so loved the world that He inspired a certain Jew to teach that there was a great deal to be said for loving your neighbour.' No. 'God so loved the world that he gave his one and only Son' (John 3:16).

FURTHER STUDY

John 15:9-13; 1 John 3:16-18

1. How does God feel about us?

2. How do we know what true love is truly like?

Those who wonder what God is really like simply have to look at the cross. The answer becomes clear: He loves to that extent! The cross reveals the nature of God and shows it to be vicarious suffering love. It pierces the darkness of this twenty-first century with a beam of light that indicates: 'This is the way into the kingdom.' It draws us – not drives us. We are won to Him by a love that personally overcomes our antipathy, and overwhelms all our suspicion and distrust. Hallelujah!

Lord Jesus, Your relentless love has cornered my soul. Help me not to reject Your redemption but to receive it in its fullness this very day. For Your name's sake. Amen.

Alive for evermore

FOR READING & MEDITATION – MATTHEW 28:1-10
'He is not here; he has risen, just as he said.' (v.6)

Having thought about the cross and its relation to the kingdom we ask ourselves: what does the resurrection of Christ really mean in terms of the kingdom of God? It is God's seal of acceptance of Christ's sacrifice made on our behalf on the cross.

Yesterday we said that God does not drive us into His kingdom by sheer force but chooses rather to draw us into His kingdom by sacrificial love. The resurrection is positive proof that God's love is as strong as His power. Had Jesus not come back from the dead then we would have always been in doubt as to whether or not God's love has any real power. It would have meant that the inhabitants of the universe would have held for ever a picture in their minds of God's love writhing on the cross in the grip of something more powerful – evil. The answer of the resurrection is No! It demonstrates that not only is God's love the most beautiful thing in heaven and earth, but it is all-powerful too. The worst man could do was matched by the best God could do, and the result was the greatest victory ever witnessed in the universe – the victory of love over sin, of goodness over evil, and of life over death.

FURTHER STUDY

Acts 2:22-41;
Rom. 1:1-4

1. Why could death not keep its hold on Jesus?

2. What did the resurrection declare?

Had the resurrection not taken place then the world would have talked of the Christian failure rather than the Christian faith. But on the first Easter morning it was the guards who 'became like dead men' (Matt 28:4) and the One supposedly guarded became 'alive for ever and ever!' (Rev. 1:18). As we think about the resurrection let us rejoice that because Jesus lives we live also. Really *live*. With the hymn writer J.S.B. Monsell we can say: 'Christ is risen! Henceforth never death or hell shall us enthral.'

Blessed Jesus and victorious Lord, how thrilled I am to know that You are alive for ever more – and that I am alive in You. Hallelujah!

Why Jesus stayed

FOR READING & MEDITATION - ACTS 1:1-5

'He appeared to them over a period of forty days and spoke
about the kingdom of God.' (v.3)

After the resurrection Jesus remained on earth for 40 days before returning to heaven. During these days He appeared to His disciples a number of times. He appeared to them when they were gathered together behind locked doors (John 20:19-29), and on the shore of the Sea of Galilee (John 21:1-22). He was also seen by 500 believers at the same time (1 Cor. 15:6). No doubt there were other appearances too.

The question you may be asking is: why did Jesus stay for 40 days? One would have thought that following His ordeal on the cross He would have been eager to return to heaven and celebrate His victory in glory. But no, He stayed 40 days here on earth with His beloved disciples. What glorious days they must have been! The disciples lived from day to day with the hope that any moment Jesus would appear to them and give further proof that He was alive. The reason why He stayed those 40 days is found in today's text: to provide strong convincing evidence that He was alive and to speak about the kingdom of God. Why was this important? Because if the disciples had wrong ideas concerning the kingdom of God then it was highly probable that all who came after them would have false ideas too. The future of the Church depended on Christ making His disciples understand the truth about His kingdom, and so He stayed with them to teach them all that they needed to know. The whole plan of salvation which Christ had worked out through His life, death and resurrection needed to be comprehended by the disciples so that they could continue His work. So He remained with them to speak with them 'of the things pertaining to the kingdom of God' (v.3, NKJV).

FURTHER STUDY

Matt. 28:16-20;
1 Cor. 15:3-24

1. What were Christ's final instructions?

2. What would have made our preaching useless?

How gracious and considerate is Your love, dear Lord. You stayed on earth those 40 days to share with Your disciples the truths of the kingdom. Yet knowing You as I do, nothing surprises me. Your love and concern is beyond compare. Amen.

Reducing the kingdom

FOR READING & MEDITATION - ACTS 1:6-8

'So when they met together, they asked him, "Lord, are you at this time going to restore the kingdom to Israel?"' (v.6)

The passage we have read today describes the meeting of Christ with His disciples in the hours before He departed from this earth. The disciples, familiar with the teaching of the Old Testament and Jesus' teaching concerning the kingdom of God, wondered if He would now usher in the kingdom, overthrow the Romans, and restore the rule once more to Israel. It is obvious that even after three years of close companionship with Jesus, and despite having absorbed His clear instruction concerning the kingdom of God, they still failed to see that what was about to happen was not the establishment of the kingdom of Israel but an event far more significant.

FURTHER STUDY

Acts 15:1-21;
Eph. 2:11-19

1. How did some believers try to reduce the kingdom?

2. What were the views of James, Peter and Paul?

We cannot blame the disciples too much for this misunderstanding, of course. It was only natural that they thought of the kingdom in terms of the kingdom of their father David. They did not reject the kingdom – they simply reduced it. The rejection of Jesus by His own people meant that the kingdom was to include not just Jews but Gentiles also. Eventually the disciples came to see this, but at this point they failed to do so because they were trying to condense the kingdom so that it fitted into their own nationalistic mould.

We do something similar every time we take the kingdom of God and try to condense it so that it fits into our denominations. 'Denominationalism,' said D.M. Panton, 'is taking the kingdom of God and turning it into the kingdom of our father David. Luther announces the kingdom of God; his followers announce the kingdom of our father Luther. Wesley announces the kingdom of God; his followers announce the kingdom of our father Wesley.' Reducing the kingdom is almost as bad as rejecting it.

O God, although I appreciate the blessings and safeguards that a denomination provides, save me from becoming denominational in my outlook, and help me see that Your kingdom is bigger than men or movements. In Jesus' name. Amen.

The inner dynamic

FOR READING & MEDITATION - ACTS 1:9-14

'They all joined constantly in prayer, along with the women and Mary the mother of Jesus, and with his brothers.' (v.14)

Two days ago we said that the whole plan of salvation which Jesus had worked out through His life, death and resurrection needed to be comprehended by His disciples so that they could continue His work. How were they enabled to fulfil their commission to continue His ministry on earth? The Day of Pentecost provides the answer.

The disciples, after the resurrection, began to understand the truths about God, Jesus, and the kingdom of God in a new way. Yet these truths were still slightly obscure and had not yet been fully perceived. The position of the disciples can be compared to that of a modern motor car which has no fuel in the tank. This is why Christ said to them: 'I am going to send you what my Father has promised; but stay in the city until you have been clothed with power from on high' (Luke 24:49). Everything was ready for the kingdom of God to come in power. The disciples, however, needed to open themselves to the inner dynamic of the Holy Spirit so that they could fulfil their mission.

Without the empowering of the Spirit the activities of the disciples would have simply been a matter of human enthusiasm combined with an effort of the will. But with the Holy Spirit flowing through them everything would be possible – and nothing impossible. The same power that worked in Jesus Christ had to work in them, and the ten days in which they waited prior to Pentecost provided them with the opportunity to lay aside their self-centredness and prepare themselves for the same flow of the Spirit which energised and motivated the life of their Lord.

FURTHER STUDY

Acts 2:1-21, 41; 4:31

1. What happened at Pentecost?

2. What happened several days later?

Lord, fill me with that self-same Spirit so that my whole life will be energised by Your power, and my ways controlled by Your love. In Jesus' name. Amen.

The kingdom in miniature

FOR READING & MEDITATION – MARK 9:1-10

'... some who are standing here will not taste death before
they see the kingdom of God come with power.' (v.1)

Before going any further we pause to focus on the words
found in today's text, which relate to the coming of the
kingdom. What did Jesus have in mind when He made this
puzzling statement? Various suggestions have been made
as to the meaning of this declaration. Some say it referred
to His transfiguration which was shortly to take place.
Others say it referred to His crucifixion and resurrection.
I myself believe Jesus was referring to the descent of the
Holy Spirit at Pentecost which initiated the spread of
Christianity throughout the Roman empire.

FURTHER STUDY

Acts 2:42-47;
5:12-16

1. How was the Early Church the kingdom in miniature?

2. How did people respond?

Following Pentecost the Church was, in the
words of the commentator Vincent Taylor, the
'visible manifestation of the rule of God displayed
in the life of an elect community'. Although the
kingdom and the Church are not identical there
is an inseparable relationship. The apostles went
about preaching the kingdom of God (see Acts
8:12; 19:8) and revealed the true nature of the
kingdom. In other words, the Church is intended
to be the kingdom in miniature. Divine power was
released at Pentecost which produced individuals
who delighted in serving God not from a sense
of compulsion but from sheer love. They showed
what it is like to be a member of God's kingdom, that is, to
submit to the rule of God.

The power that surged through the hearts of those
disciples following Pentecost is with us today and, despite
all appearances to the contrary, is shaping the course of
history in preparation for the day when all the kingdoms
of the world will finally be brought under the absolute
sovereignty of our Lord and Saviour Jesus Christ.

**Gracious Father, strengthen me so that I become a vital part of
Your kingdom. Through my life and witness may others come to
accept Your rule and reign as their constant way of life. In Jesus'
name. Amen.**

Still Waters

What picture of God do you carry deep in your heart? How you answer that question will have a significant bearing on how you live your life, particularly when faced with any form of upheaval.

In the next issue, Selwyn takes us phrase by phrase through one of the best-loved passages of Scripture – Psalm 23 – a psalm which describes in vivid language God's character and His care for us, as a shepherd cares for his sheep.

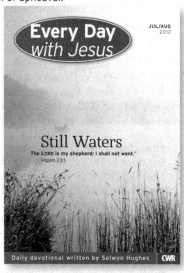

Topics considered include:
· Finding God's perspective on life
· Facing fear
· Discovering the source of spiritual strength

OBTAIN YOUR COPY FROM
CWR, a Christian bookshop or National Distributor.
If you would like to take out a subscription, see the order form at the back of these notes.

The keys of the kingdom

FOR READING & MEDITATION - MATTHEW 16:13-20

'I will give you the keys of the kingdom of heaven; whatever you bind on earth will be bound in heaven ...' (v.19)

Yesterday we made the comment that the Church is the kingdom of God in miniature. The kingdom is working through the Church. In the text before us today Jesus says that He will give the keys of the kingdom to His Church and thus provide the Church with the power to bind and to loose. Just what are these 'keys' which Jesus talks about here?

We get a glimpse of what was in Jesus' mind when we turn to Luke 11:52: 'Woe to you experts in the law, because you have taken away the key to knowledge. You yourselves have not entered, and you have hindered those who were entering.' The key to understanding the purposes of God for the world had been given to Israel, but the teachers had misinterpreted the oracles of God to such a degree that when the Messiah came among them they did not recognise Him. Paul, you may remember, told the Romans that the Jews had been entrusted 'with the very words of God' (Rom. 3:2). However, such was the blindness in the eyes of the teachers of the law that they failed to enter the kingdom and, what was worse, hindered others from entering also. So the keys, along with the blessings of the kingdom, were given to a new people, the Church, to loose men and women from their sins.

FURTHER STUDY

Acts 10:34-48;
Eph. 3:1-12

1. What key did Peter use?

2. What key did Paul reveal?

The kingdom which came into the world in the Person of Christ and is now working through the Church will one day be fully established and acknowledged when Christ comes again in great power and glory. I hope your heart responds as mine does when I reflect on these tremendous truths. Let us echo the prayer found in the closing chapter of the book of Revelation: 'Even so, come, Lord Jesus!' (Rev. 22:20, NKJV).

Father, I am so grateful that I am a participant in Your purposes, and a member of this unending kingdom. Help us as Your Church to be a true witness to all nations by our prayers, our giving and our total commitment. In Jesus' name. Amen.

FOR READING & MEDITATION - ACTS 19:1-12

'Paul ... spoke boldly ... arguing persuasively about the kingdom of
God. But some ... publicly maligned the Way.' (vv.8-9)

In the account of Paul's time in Ephesus the terms 'the
kingdom of God' and 'the Way' (which is the Church) are
used synonymously. Though the kingdom of God extends
beyond the Church since its field of operation includes all
of God's redeeming activity in the world, the Church is the
one visible manifestation of the kingdom.

It was necessary for God to make clear to men and women
the true nature of the kingdom for, despite the teaching
given in the Old Testament, people failed to understand
its principles and follow its precepts. If Jesus, for example,
had simply been proclaimed as the Way without
that Way being incarnate in a human form then
the whole plan of salvation would have been
ineffective. The Way became flesh, and through a
human form Christ showed God to us and shared
God with us. It is the same with the kingdom. Had
the kingdom been proclaimed verbally as the Way
then it would have failed to move people. So just as
the Word became flesh in Jesus, the Way became
flesh in the Church. Both the divine Person and
the divine order were needed to complete the
picture of God's kingdom.

In the Church we see both the Person and
the order at work, providing us with an idea of what the
kingdom of God is like on a universal scale. The Acts of
the Apostles is not just the portrayal of the Early Church;
it is that – and more! It is an exploration of the order and
nature of the kingdom of God – the kingdom that now is
and the kingdom that is to be. In order that we might see
what the kingdom of God is like on a cosmic scale God has
graciously given us a glimpse of it in His Church.

FURTHER STUDY

John 14:1-6;
13:5; 1 Pet.
2:21-25

1. In what sense
is Jesus the way
to salvation?

2. In what sense
is Jesus the
way to live?

**Lord, though we are grateful for principles, what our hearts crave
for is a Person. We need a heart to answer our own hearts. In You
we have found the answer to our deepest needs. And for this we
are truly thankful. Amen.**

The new society

'And the Lord added to their number daily those who were being saved.' (v.47)

We have been saying that the Church is the kingdom of God in miniature. Just as Jesus' kingdom is not of this world (John 18:36) so the Church is separate from the world. Those who belong to it accept Christ as their ruler and are God's way of introducing the ideal order of things – they have been given the responsibility of extending God's kingdom on earth.

One commentator, G.E. Ladd, made the point that the kingdom of God created the Church. This is how he put it: 'The redemptive rule of God brings into being a new people who receive the blessings of the divine reign. Furthermore, it was the activity of the divine rule which brought judgement upon Israel. Historically, the activity of the kingdom of God effected the creation of the Church and the destruction of Israel.' Some believe that the verse we looked at the other day in which Jesus said, '... some who are standing here will not taste death before they see the kingdom of God come with power' (Mark 9:1), has reference to this. Whether or not it does, there can be no doubt that within the lifetime of the disciples the kingdom of God would bring about great judgment on Jerusalem as well as creating the new society known as the Church.

FURTHER STUDY

Acts 4:32-37;
11:27-30;
Col. 3:15-17;
1 Tim. 5:1-3

1. What are the characteristics of the new society?

2. What binds all virtues together?

What a thrilling picture Scripture presents to us when it shows the kingdom working through the Church. In future when you read through any section of the Acts of the Apostles keep in mind that what you are reading about is not only the Church in action (exciting though that is) but the kingdom at work through the Church. Think of it like this: the Church to which we belong has cosmic backing. How wonderful. How truly wonderful.

Yes Father, it is truly wonderful. Flowing through Your Church is the energy of a universal and unshakeable kingdom. I am part of a cosmic purpose. What a privilege. All honour and glory be to Your wonderful name. Amen.

FOR READING & MEDITATION - PSALM 16:1-11

'I have set the LORD always before me. Because he is at my right hand, I shall not be shaken.' (v.8)

The Church of Jesus Christ, which is part of the kingdom of God and exists now in time, is, however, not of this world. It is a society within a society, a nation within a nation, and a people within a people. When the nations around us decay and fall into ruin because of their unwillingness to live according to the laws of God then the Church will still stand fast because it has been bought with the cross of Jesus (Acts 20:28) and has a God-given role to play. Its purpose in this world is to be the expression of the kingdom of God and to demonstrate to the nations of the earth that it belongs to a kingdom that cannot be shaken. As we have already noted, Jesus promised that 'the gates of Hades will not overcome it' (Matt. 16:18).

The pastor of a large church on the West Coast of America found that the congregation swelled by several thousand in the weeks following the traumatic events that took place in New York and Washington on 11 September 2001. Naturally he was interested to know just why there were so many newcomers in the Sunday and mid-week services. As a result of gentle questioning he discovered the following reasons: the first was that people felt a need to get their lives straightened out spiritually, and the second that they were drawn to this particular church because of the calmness they had noticed in those who worshipped there.

What an opportunity we have at this time, when so much around us is being shaken, to show the men and women of the world that although we react to tragedies with the same shock and dismay as they do, inwardly we are possessed by a core of calmness and poise that nothing can shatter.

FURTHER STUDY

Exod. 14:10-31; Mark 4:35-41

1. Contrast Moses and the Israelites.

2. Contrast Jesus and the disciples.

O Father, I am so grateful for this inner reinforcement that enables me to have a peace and confidence that nothing can destroy. For that I praise and thank You. Amen.

We see Jesus

One of the great missionary hymns of the Christian Church begins with the words: 'Jesus shall reign where'er the sun doth his successive journeys run' – a brave note to sing in these dark days when the authority of Christ is so widely denied. While we recognise the fact that Isaac Watts, the hymnist, was looking forward to the time when the rule of Christ will be unchallenged by the whole universe, we must also see that the New Testament teaches not so much that Jesus *shall* reign as that He *does* reign.

To the writers of the New Testament letters the kingship of Christ was not something in the future about which they could speculate, but rather something in the present that they could enjoy. This truth is brought out best by the writer to the Hebrews who says: '... we see Jesus ... crowned.' We *see* – not, we shall see. It was not the faint hope that Jesus would one day occupy the throne which sustained and inspired the early Christians in their struggle against the evil forces which surrounded them, but the sure knowledge that Christ was on the throne – crowned, glorified and triumphant.

FURTHER STUDY

John 18:33-40;
Eph. 1:15-22

1. What did Jesus acknowledge?

2. What did Paul acknowledge?

You and I, in these difficult days through which the world is passing, need a similar assurance. We too need to see that Jesus really reigns in the midst of this worldwide confusion, and that all that is subject to His overarching plan. Everything that happens God can use. It is important to our faith that we are convinced of the present personal sovereignty of Christ and not just of the eventual triumph of His cause. Despite appearances to the contrary, Jesus is even now supreme. He is seated there right now – on the throne!

O God, thank You for showing me that in this dark age through which I am passing You are not struggling to make Your way to the throne. You are already there. Hallelujah!

The devil's crown

FOR READING & MEDITATION - LUKE 4:1-13

'And he said to him, "I will give you all their authority and splendour,
for it has been given to me ..."' (v.6)

Yesterday we said that despite all appearances to the
contrary Jesus is seated right now on the throne of His
Father, and is ruling over the affairs of men. Over the next
few days we are going to examine Jesus' unique position as
King of kings and Lord of lords.

The Scriptures tell us that on two separate occasions
during His earthly life Jesus was offered a crown. The first
occasion was during His temptation in the desert when
the devil took Him to a high place and offered Him all the
kingdoms of the world. Our reading today presents us with
the details of what must have been one of the
most dramatic moments in the life of Christ. As
all legal rights to the kingdoms of the earth had
been forfeited by Adam when he sinned, control
over the earth had to a great extent passed into the
devil's hands. Here Satan is seen offering Jesus a
means whereby He could obtain the kingdoms of
the world without difficulty or delay. No cross, no
pain, no agony, no shame – how easy it all could
have been! Why did not Jesus close with the offer
and accept the crown from the devil's hands?

The reason is simple: Jesus would not attempt to
achieve the divine end by any means other than
the divine method. If Satan's dominion over the
kingdoms of the earth was to be revoked then
it must be done without violating the universal
principles of justice on which the universe had
been founded. And not only must justice be done, but it
must be seen to be done. In rejecting Satan's offer Christ
demonstrated His willingness to follow God's plan to the
letter – even though it meant the pain and shame of
the cross.

FURTHER STUDY

Matt. 26:36-39;
Heb. 10:1-23;
11:24-26

1. What conflicting choices and desires did Christ experience?

2. Why may pain be more important than pleasure?

**Lord Jesus, everything You did while You were here on earth
was done with me in mind. You resisted every temptation and
overcame every conflict so that I could belong to Your kingdom. I
am truly thankful. Amen.**

The people's crown

FOR READING & MEDITATION – JOHN 6:15-21

'Jesus, knowing that they intended to come and make him king by force, withdrew again to a mountain by himself.' (v.15)

The second time Jesus was offered a crown while He was here on earth it was the people who tried to give it to Him. By this stage in His ministry Jesus had become enormously popular, and everywhere He went adoring crowds followed Him. Inspired by His miraculous works and mighty words, His countrymen resolved to take Him by force and make Him a king. Yet He refused to have anything to do with their plan. When they came to crown Him He took evasive action and withdrew to a mountain.

Why did Jesus decline this honour? Some have suggested He perceived that the attachment of the crowds was shallow and transitory, and that though at that time they applauded Him, before long they would treat Him not as a king but as a criminal. But there was another and far deeper reason. It was this: the kingdom which Christ intended to establish was not to be an earthly kingdom bounded by frontiers and peopled only by members of the Jewish race; it was to be a universal kingdom reaching to the four corners of the earth and encompassing the whole of the human race. A kingdom founded by the use of physical force was unacceptable to the Son of God for had He wished to establish His kingdom on that basis then He need never have left His home in heaven. He had come not simply to show God's omnipotent power but God's almighty love.

This is why centuries after the 'glory that was Greece and the grandeur that was Rome' have passed away, the kingdom of God stands as secure as ever. It is founded on the imperishable love of God, and as such it is as unshakeable as God's eternal throne.

FURTHER STUDY

John 10:14-18;
Acts 13:47-49

1. What did Jesus explain?

2. What did the apostles understand about Christ?

Blessed Lord Jesus, I am amazed by Your self-sacrifice and eternal love. As I ponder Your ways while You were here on earth I feel that I am on holy ground. And every bush is aflame with Your love. Amen.

The Father's crown

FOR READING & MEDITATION – HEBREWS 2:6-10

'Yet at present we do not see everything subject to him.' (v.8)

Today we think a little more about the crown which has been offered to Jesus by His Father – the crown we first mentioned three days ago. The fact that Jesus has accepted this crown and is already reigning raises a problem in the minds of many Christians and they say: 'If Jesus Christ is King of kings and Lord of lords then why do we see so many things happening in the world which are directly contrary to His will, such as wars, famine, and poverty?'

The words 'Yet at present we do not see everything subject to him' refer not to Jesus but to man who having been given dominion over the earth in the Garden of Eden surrendered the legal rights to Satan when he sinned and stepped outside of God's original plan. Although Jesus has returned to heaven and wears the crown of universal authority, He has not dramatically intervened in human affairs to sweep away all resistance to His will and force men and women to capitulate to His demands. He is working patiently with them to restore to them the dominion lost by Adam, and this part of His purposes is being carried out by His redeemed people – the Church.

FURTHER STUDY

2 Pet. 3:1-9;
Rev. 17:12-14

1. Why may the Lord appear slow to assert full authority?

2. Who will be with the King of kings?

Although Christ is King and has absolute authority over all things, He is at this present moment using world conditions as on-the-job training for His Church. 'Do you not know', said Paul, 'that we will judge angels?' (I Cor. 6:3). God is proceeding in His world according to a divine timetable, and one reason (though not, of course, the only one) why He does not assert His authority and overcome all resistance to His will is because He is preparing you and me – His redeemed people – to rule with Him in His coming kingdom.

O God, how foolish I have been to doubt Your sovereignty. May I be able to say with complete assurance: 'God is working His purpose out, as year succeeds to year.' In Jesus' name. Amen.

Our apprenticeship

FOR READING & MEDITATION - EPHESIANS 6:10-18

'... put on the full armour of God, so that when the day of evil comes, you may be able to stand your ground ...' (v.13)

Yesterday we said that God has given Jesus Christ a crown of authority and power. He alone has the title of 'KING OF KINGS AND LORD OF LORDS' (Rev. 19:16). Do you see what follows from this? If Jesus has received His sovereignty from neither Satan nor men then neither Satan nor men can deprive Him of it! He wears the crown eternally. No one can dethrone Him! What a heartening thought this is – Jesus does reign!

As we have already observed, some of the things that happen in the world may cause us to question Christ's supremacy and power, yet we know from the teaching found in the Scriptures that God's great redemptive plan has been set in motion. What possible purpose can God have in allowing the power of Satan to continue, along with that of the millions of evil spirits that are loose in the world? Well, the answer is, on one level, quite simple and we touched on it yesterday. At this stage in history the Church of Jesus Christ is being trained for the position that one day will be ours. While waiting for Jesus to return we are passing through a period of apprenticeship during which we are being prepared for the time when we 'will reign for ever and ever' (Rev. 22:5) in company with the crowned King of heaven – our Lord and Saviour Jesus Christ.

FURTHER STUDY

Eph. 1:15-23;
2 Cor. 10:1-5;
James 4:7

1. What power has God given us?

2. What are we able to do?

God is bent on showing us something of the tremendous power and authority we have in prayer which, according to Paul, is mighty to the pulling down of the strongholds of Satan. When we, as God's people, begin to see the real purpose of our apprenticeship then perhaps we will be that much nearer to bringing back the King.

Teach me the art of spiritual warfare, dear Lord, so that I might serve my apprenticeship with honour. This I ask in Christ's name and for His glory. Amen.

Jesus shall reign

FOR READING & MEDITATION - 1 CORINTHIANS 15:22-28

'For he must reign until he has put all his enemies under his feet.'

(v.25)

Does it seem to you that present world conditions are a refutation of our Master's regal claims? Is He really reigning from the throne? To show how different attitudes can be I have selected two stories relating to historical figures.

In the late sixteenth and early seventeenth centuries a theologian, Andrew Melville, was a champion of the Scottish Church. His chief concern was that the Church should be independent of state control. One day, angered by unwarranted interference in ecclesiastical affairs, he walked unbidden into the presence of James VI and said: 'Sir, as divers times before I have told you, so now again I must tell you, there are two kings and two kingdoms in Scotland: there is King James, the head of this commonwealth, and there is Christ Jesus, the King of the Church, whose subject James the Sixth is, and of whose kingdom he is not a king, nor a lord, nor a head, but a member.'

The attitude of Queen Victoria three centuries later was very different. When she was well advanced in years she is reported to have said following a sermon on the second coming of Jesus Christ: 'My supreme desire is to live until the second coming of the Lord so that I may present to Him with my own hands the kingdoms of Great Britain and Ireland.'

Grasp this reassuring truth and let it hold you as you move forward in these dark days: Jesus does reign now in His Church and shall reign at the predetermined time of God's appointment over all the kingdoms of the universe. Let there be no doubt about it: the consequences of His conquest at Calvary will spread like ripples in a pond until He has put every enemy under His feet.

FURTHER STUDY

Dan. 4:28-37;
Rev. 19:11-21

1. What did Nebuchad-nezzar come to realise?

2. What is the end of those who oppose Christ's reign?

Gracious God, however things may seem, may I never forget that You are truly the Lord of the universe and that Satan is a defeated foe. In Jesus' name I ask this. Amen.

A time for concern

FOR READING & MEDITATION – MATTHEW 6:5-15

'... your kingdom come, your will be done on earth
as it is in heaven.' (v.10)

The question that confronts us now is this: how is the kingdom of God to come on earth as it is in heaven? The kingdom is established as the will of God is done in the social, religious and political affairs of the world, just as it is done in heaven. God's kingdom has come wherever His rule is being acknowledged. The Church's commission is to extend the kingdom, and it should be demonstrating to the world something of the nature of the kingdom as it daily carries out the will of God in its affairs.

When we see what a tremendous part the Church has to play in world affairs by being the expression of the will of God on earth then we need wonder no longer why it is that the lack of unity among believers brings such pain to the heart of God. The next time we pray 'Your kingdom come, your will be done on earth as it is in heaven' let us make sure that we do not deny with our lives what we say with our lips. The scandal of the universe is the constant bickering that goes on between believers who profess to be followers of the one Lord Jesus Christ. Shame on us brothers! Shame on us sisters! The world is breaking up around us, and is disintegrating because of its failure to live by the laws that bind life together, yet we the people of God hold on to our grievances, nurse our hostilities, and refuse to forgive – even though we know that this grieves God and causes sorrow in the heart of Jesus.

FURTHER STUDY

1 Cor. 6:1-8;
Gal. 5:22-26

1. How should we handle disagreements?

2. What is the antidote to bickering?

I urge the many thousands of you who are reading these lines today to join with me in repenting before God for this tragic insensitivity. Let us ask Him to give us a spiritual revival that will make its impact felt throughout every branch of the Church and into the world.

With all my heart, dear Lord, I plead and pray for a worldwide revival to cross the continents and engulf the world. I repent of my insensitivity and ask Your forgiveness. In Jesus' name. Amen.

FOR READING & MEDITATION - MATTHEW 5:13-16

'You are the light of the world. A city on a hill cannot be hidden.' (v.14)

We have one more question to consider: how can we who are members of the unshakeable kingdom interpret to the world the claims of Christ our King? How are we to proclaim His kingship? Are we to wait until Jesus Himself returns in triumph and manifests His regal power? No, we can make His claims known now by our lips, by our lives and by our liberality. Apart from the obvious need to witness for Jesus Christ in our daily contacts with the unconverted, we must take a stance on the many issues affecting today's society.

When considering a particular issue we must ask ourselves what attitude we should take. How do we represent our King in our modern society? Hugh Price Hughes said: 'It is the Christian's business to make himself a public nuisance until every other public nuisance is cleared away.' We must watch, however, that we do not simply become reactionaries; rather, we should be revolutionaries. 'Why is it', asks a missionary working in South America, 'that when the Church speaks out on social issues it is usually against what is happening? Our task, rather, is to speak out on issues before the world gets around to thinking about them.'

FURTHER STUDY

Eph. 5:1-21;
1 Thess. 5:4-8

1. How may our light shine?

2. How may our light be hidden?

Is it not an indictment against us that the Church of Jesus Christ, which started out as the most revolutionary movement in the world, has descended to the level of being the most reactionary establishment in today's society? Herbert Agar was right when, in his book *A Time for Greatness*, he said: 'The supreme need of the hour is not for one or two outstanding figures of vision and initiative, but for high living and high thinking on the part of the common people.'

O God, may I be a revolutionary and not a reactionary so that by my life and through my speech I can present the claims of Your kingdom to the society in which I live. This I ask in Christ's name. Amen.

Beyond all telling

FOR READING & MEDITATION - REVELATION 22:1-5

'And they will reign for ever and ever.' (v.5)

On this our last day together we look back over the past two months to think about the lessons we have learned. We have seen that the kingdom of God is the rule of God – anywhere – and having considered its principles and pattern we are spoiled for any other kind of society. God's kingdom, which Adam rebelled against, has been regained in Christ, and offered not to one particular nation or race but to those gathered from all nations and races who willingly surrender their lives to the Lord Jesus Christ.

Once we have accepted Jesus Christ as Lord we are joined with that part of His kingdom known as the Church, which is the kingdom of God in miniature. God's purpose for the Church is to extend the kingdom on earth by submitting to His will. In this way the Church shows the world what life is like when God's laws are obeyed and His principles are followed. God's long-term plan is not to sustain this flawed society where children are poor and starved and where the weak are exploited by the strong. Instead He will sweep away the foundations on which such societies are founded and make way for the kingdom that cannot be shaken.

FURTHER STUDY

Isa. 65:17-25;
Rev. 21:1-7,22-27

1. What is the future like?

2. Who will inherit this future?

Despite all appearances to the contrary, the kingdom of God is gradually being established in this world. As Jesus taught in the parables of the mustard seed and the yeast, it will grow amazingly and invade our evil environment (Matt. 13:31–33). Then, when the King returns triumphantly on the clouds of heaven, it will finally be manifested to all people. For those who belong to the Church, the future is beyond all telling. Our destiny is to reign with God and Christ for ever and ever – world without end.

Lord Jesus, help me from this day forward to extend Your kingdom and apply the principles of the kingdom to every area of life. And, through Your wondrous grace, may I move into the future without fear, strong in faith and courage. Amen.

4 EASY WAYS TO ORDER:

1. Phone in your credit card order: **01252 784710** (Mon–Fri, 9.30am–5pm)

2. Visit our Online Store at **www.cwr.org.uk/store**

3. Send this form together with your payment to:
   CWR, Waverley Abbey House, Waverley Lane, Farnham, Surrey GU9 8EP

4. Visit your local Christian bookshop

a list of our National Distributors, who supply countries outside the UK, visit www.cwr.org.uk/distributors

OUR DETAILS (REQUIRED FOR ORDERS AND DONATIONS)

ame:	**CWR ID No.** (if known):
ome Address:	
	Postcode:
lephone No. (for queries):	**Email:**

UBLICATIONS

TITLE	QTY	PRICE	TOTAL
		Total publications	

p&p: up to £24.99 = **£2.99**; £25.00 and over = **FREE**

ewhere **p&p:** up to £10 = **£4.95**; £10.01 – £50 = **£6.95**; £50.01 – £99.99 = **£10**; £100 and over = **£30**

ase allow 14 days for delivery

Total publications and p&p **A**	

UBSCRIPTIONS* (NON DIRECT DEBIT)

	QTY	PRICE (INCLUDING P&P)			TOTAL
		UK	**Europe**	**Elsewhere**	
ry Day with Jesus (1yr, 6 issues)		£15.50	£19.25	Please contact nearest National Distributor or CWR direct	
ge Print Every Day with Jesus (1yr, 6 issues)		£15.50	£19.25		
piring Women Every Day (1yr, 6 issues)		£15.50	£19.25		
Every Day (Jeff Lucas) (1yr, 6 issues)		£15.50	£19.25		
er to Cover Every Day (1yr, 6 issues)		£15.50	£19.25		
tle: 14–18s (1yr, 3 issues)		£13.80	£15.90		
s: 11–15s (1yr, 6 issues)		£15.50	£19.25		
z: 7–11s (1yr, 6 issues)		£15.50	£19.25		

Total Subscriptions (Subscription prices already include postage and packing) **B**	

circle which bimonthly issue you would like your subscription to commence from:
eb Mar/Apr May/Jun Jul/Aug Sep/Oct Nov/Dec

use this section for subscriptions paid for by credit/debit card or
que. For Direct Debit subscriptions see overleaf.

CONTINUED OVERLEAF >>

PAYMENT DETAILS

☐ I enclose a cheque/PO made payable to CWR for the amount of: **£** _____

☐ Please charge my credit/debit card.

Cardholder's name (in BLOCK CAPITALS) _____

Card No. ☐☐☐☐ ☐☐☐☐ ☐☐☐☐ ☐☐☐☐ ☐☐☐☐

Expires end ☐☐☐☐   Security Code ☐☐☐

GIFT TO CWR (TMW PRISON APPPEAL)

☐ Please send me an acknowledgement of my gift   **C** ☐

GIFT AID (YOUR HOME ADDRESS REQUIRED, SEE OVERLEAF)

giftaid it

I am a UK taxpayer and want CWR to reclaim the tax on all my donations for the four years prior to this year **and on** all donations I make from the date of this Gift Aid declaration until further notice.*

Taxpayer's Full Name (in BLOCK CAPITALS) _____

Signature _____ **Date** _____

*I understand I must pay an amount of Income/Capital Gains Tax at least equal to the tax the charity reclaims in the tax year.

GRAND TOTAL (Total of A, B, & C) ☐

SUBSCRIPTIONS BY DIRECT DEBIT (UK BANK ACCOUNT HOLDERS ONLY)

Subscriptions cost £15.50 (except *Mettle*: £13.80) for one year for delivery within the UK. Please tick relevant boxes and fill in the fo

☐ *Every Day with Jesus* (1yr, 6 issues)
☐ Large Print *Every Day with Jesus* (1yr, 6 issues)
☐ *Inspiring Women Every Day* (1yr, 6 issues)
☐ *Life Every Day* (Jeff Lucas) (1yr, 6 issues)

☐ *Cover to Cover Every Day* (1yr, 6 issues)
☐ *Mettle*: 14-18s (1yr, 3 issues)
☐ *YP's*: 11-15s (1yr, 6 issues)
☐ *Topz*: 7-11s (1yr, 6 issues)

Issue to commenc
☐ Jan/Feb ☐ Jul/A
☐ Mar/Apr ☐ Sep/O
☐ May/Jun ☐ Nov/I

CWR

Instruction to your Bank or Building Society to pay by Direct Debit

DIRE **Deb**

Please fill in the form and send to: CWR, Waverley Abbey House, Waverley Lane, Farnham, Surrey GU9 8EP

Name and full postal address of your Bank or Building Society

To: The Manager _____ Bank/Building Society

Address _____

_____ Postcode _____

Name(s) of Account Holder(s)

_____

Branch Sort Code ☐☐ ☐☐ ☐☐

Bank/Building Society account number ☐☐☐☐☐☐☐☐

Originator's Identification Number

| 4 | 2 | 0 | 4 | 8 | 7 |

Reference

☐☐☐☐☐☐☐☐☐☐☐☐☐☐

Instruction to your Bank or Building Society

Please pay CWR Direct Debits from the account detailed in this Instructio to the safeguards assured by the Direct Debit Guarantee.

I understand that this Instruction may remain with CWR and, if so, details passed electronically to my Bank/Building Society.

Signature(s)

_____

Date _____

Banks and Building Societies may not accept Direct Debit Instructions for some types of account